DECORATIVE PAINT TECHNIQUES & IDEAS | MEREDITH BOOKS® | DES MOINES, IOWA

Decorative Paint Techniques & Ideas
Project Manager/Writer: Cathy Long
Art Director: The Design Office of Jerry J. Rank
Copy Chief: Terri Fredrickson
Publishing Operations Manager: Karen Schirm
Senior Editor, Asset and Information Manager: Phillip Morgan
Edit and Design Production Coordinator: Mary Lee Gavin
Editorial Assistant: Kaye Chabot
Book Production Managers: Pam Kvitne, Marjorie J. Schenkelberg,
  Rick von Holdt, Mark Weaver
Contributing Copy Editor: Amanda Knief
Contributing Proofreaders: Julie Cahalan, Nancy Ruhling, Jody Speer
Contributing Photographers: Scott Little, Blaine Moats, Jason Wilde
Decorative Painters: Patricia Mohr Kramer, Molly Spain
Stylist: Cathy Kramer
Illustrator: Barbara J. Gordon, Carson Ode
Indexer: Sharon Duffy

Meredith® Books
Executive Director, Editorial: Gregory H. Kayko
Executive Director, Design: Matt Strelecki
Senior Editor/Group Manager: Vicki Leigh Ingham
Senior Associate Design Director: Ken Carlson
Marketing Product Manager: Tyler Woods

Publisher and Editor in Chief: James D. Blume
Editorial Director: Linda Raglan Cunningham
Executive Director, New Business Development: Todd M. Davis
Executive Director, Sales: Ken Zagor
Director, Operations: George A. Susral
Director, Production: Douglas M. Johnston
Director, Marketing: Amy Nichols
Business Director: Jim Leonard

Vice President and General Manager: Douglas J. Guendel

Better Homes and Gardens® Magazine
Editor in Chief: Karol DeWulf Nickell
Deputy Editor, Home Design: Oma Blaise Ford

Meredith Publishing Group
President: Jack Griffin
Senior Vice President: Bob Mate
Meredith Corporation
Chairman and Chief Executive Officer: William T. Kerr
President and Chief Operating Officer: Stephen M. Lacy

In Memoriam: E.T. Meredith III (1933-2003)

All of us at Meredith® Books are dedicated to providing
you with information and ideas to enhance your home.
We welcome your comments and suggestions. Write to us at:
Meredith Books, Home Decorating Editorial Department, 1716
Locust St., Des Moines, IA 50309-3023.

If you would like to purchase any of our home decorating
and design, cooking, crafts, gardening, or home improvement
books, check wherever quality books are sold. Or visit us at:
bhgbooks.com

decorative paint introduction

If your walls lack depth and interest, grab a gallon of paint. Painting is the fastest and most inexpensive way to change the look and feel of a room. Painting your walls a solid color is fine, but why not take it a step further and try a decorative paint technique? Decorative painting brings a sense of richness and creativity to your room. It can be as easy as striping or combing your walls or as challenging as plastering or illusionistic trompe l'oeil painting. This book—for both the novice and experienced decorative painter—is just the tool to help you get started.

The book is divided into two sections. The first section teaches you about color selection, shows you the tools that you will need for basic painting, and takes you through the steps of preparing your walls for painting and applying that first base coat. The second section provides 50 tried-and-true paint finishes with favorites such as denim, strié, striping, color washing, and stenciling, along with popular techniques such as distressing, sponging, and aging. There also are cutting-edge techniques such as grass-cloth, wicker, Venetian plaster, wall graphics, and appliqué. The book includes detailed, step-by-step instructions and photography, as well as tips from decorative painting professionals that will help you dress your walls with success.

With this book by your side, plain walls never will be the same.
Happy painting!

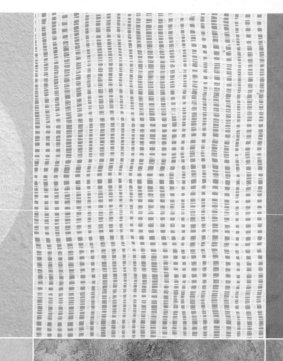

decorative paint contents

decorative paint basics

Decorative painting can be an extremely rewarding experience, but time needs to be devoted to planning and preparation before you begin. This section is designed to give you the information you need to plan your painting project with confidence.

Selecting a color scheme is one of the more challenging parts of any new decorating project. It's a good idea to have a general understanding of color principles, and the best place to start is the color wheel. The color wheel illustrates how colors relate to each other and how to combine them for a pleasing effect. To assist you in narrowing down your color selection, look for a source of inspiration—anything from an admired swatch of fabric to a favorite piece of art. Then consider taking your color palette a step further by adding pattern and texture to your finish.

This section also provides the information you need to choose the right tools for basic painting and measuring. This includes how to use each tool, and a picture so you can locate it easily at your local home center or paint store. And before you pick up a brush, read the primer on basic painting with information on how to prepare your walls for painting and tips on the easiest and fastest way to apply those first coats of paint.

This early planning phase will eliminate the guesswork when you reach that next important step—selecting the decorative paint finish that's right for you and your space.

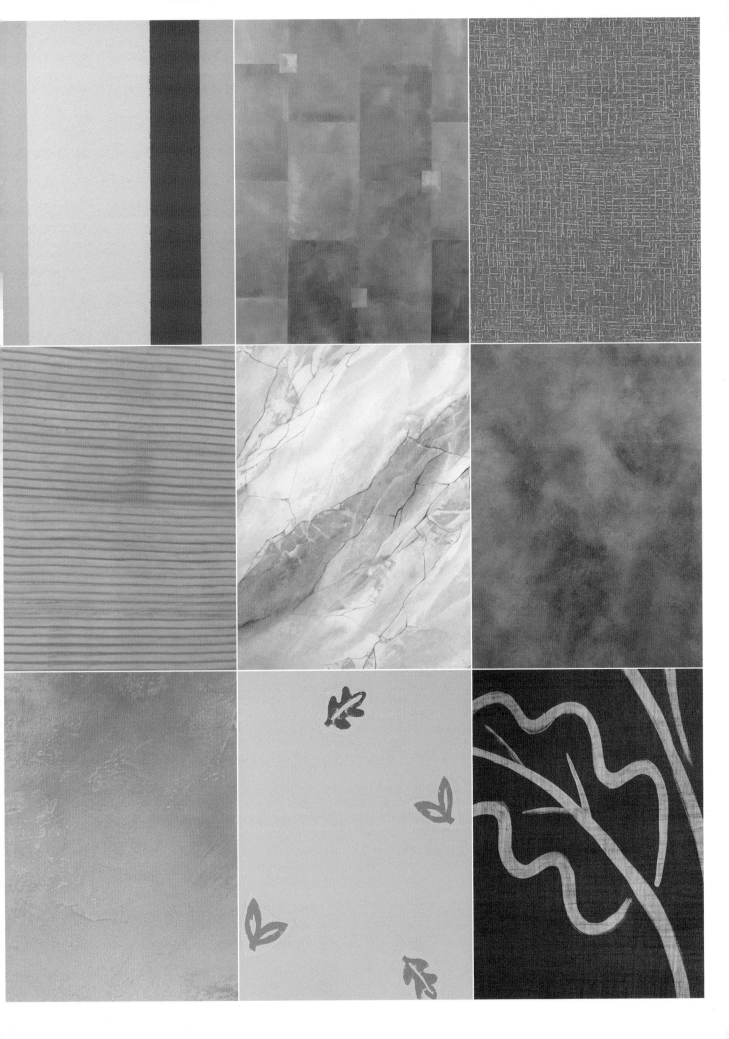

making color choices

It can be overwhelming to think about changing the decor of your home. When you do, be prepared to make a series of choices before you start your project. The first decision you need to make is the color of your walls. Color sets the mood for any room, and with so many colors to choose from, it's often hard to know where to start. You need to have a basic understanding of color theory, and the best place to start is the color wheel.

THE COLOR WHEEL

Interior designers use the color wheel and the information it provides when they make color selections for any decorating project. The color wheel shows the relationships between colors and how they affect each other to create looks that are pleasing. The color wheel is divided into three categories: primary, secondary, and tertiary.

PRIMARY COLORS

Primary colors are the first level of color. They are the three pure hues—red, yellow, and blue. These colors create all other colors. They are located at equal distances around the color wheel.

ABOUT GLAZES

GLAZING IS A POPULAR TECHNIQUE OFTEN USED BY PROFESSIONAL DECORATORS AND DO-IT-YOURSELFERS TO ADD DEFINITION TO WALLS. GLAZE IS A MILKY LIQUID THAT DRIES CLEAR. PAINT COLOR IS USED TO TINT THE GLAZE BEFORE IT'S APPLIED TO THE WALL. THE MORE GLAZE ADDED TO THE MIXTURE, THE MORE TRANSLUCENT THE EFFECT AND THE LONGER "OPEN TIME" OR WORKING TIME YOU WILL HAVE TO COMPLETE YOUR WALL FINISH. WHEN A SMALLER AMOUNT IS USED, THE EFFECT WILL BE HEAVIER AND YOU WILL HAVE LESS WORKING TIME. THE MIXTURE CAN SOMETIMES BE THINNED WITH WATER OR OTHER WETTING AGENTS TO EXTEND THE WORKING TIME. USE A STIR STICK TO PROPERLY INCORPORATE THE GLAZE MEDIUM AND THE PAINT BEFORE USING. TINTED GLAZES ARE ALSO AVAILABLE. USE THIS MEDIUM TO CREATE POPULAR DECORATIVE PAINT FINISHES SUCH AS DENIM, MOTTLED SPONGING, LINEN, AND STONE BLOCKS.

THESE 3 PRIMARY COLORS CREATE ALL OTHER COLORS

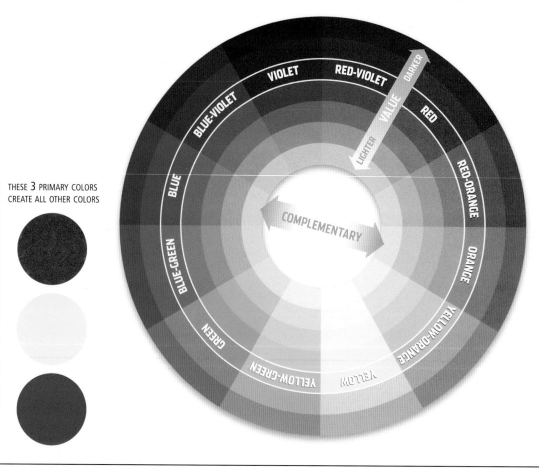

SECONDARY COLORS

Secondary colors are the second tier of color—orange, green, and violet. They are called secondary colors because they are mixed from two primary colors; for example, red and yellow make orange. Each secondary color lies between the two primaries that combine to create that color.

TERTIARY COLORS

Tertiary colors are created by mixing a secondary color and a primary color; for example, blue and violet create blue-violet.

By understanding the color wheel, the relationships between colors, and how they combine with each other and work together, you can determine which colors go well together. This will make it easier to select a palette that will work for you. Narrow your color choices by looking for inspiration.

LOOK FOR INSPIRATION

There are many sources of inspiration to help you select a pleasing color palette. To start, look through books and magazines and create a file of rooms and colors that inspire you. Find an item that you like—a fabric, a rug, a painting, a print, a pillow, or even a mug—and inspect it for information. What do you like about it? Is it the color, the texture, or the pattern? Try to figure out why it appeals to you and how to translate that to your wall. Do you want to complement the item, or do you want the room to flow around it? Answering these questions will help you as you start to build a color scheme.

SELECT A COLOR SCHEME

There are no hard and fast rules in selecting colors that harmonize with each other, but there are natural combinations of colors that look pleasing when used together.

Complementary colors are two hues that lie directly opposite each other on the color wheel. When placed next to each other, each appears more intense. Analogous colors are three colors side by side on the color wheel. In an analogous scheme one color is dominant, and the others are secondary in importance.

To build a scheme, pick up paint chips from your local paint store and cut the paint chips apart to isolate the colors that you like. Most of the choices in the color deck are tints, tones, and shades of the three primary colors. The color deck will give you warm choices (reds, yellows, and oranges), cool choices (blues, violets, greens), and neutral choices (browns, grays, black, and shades of white). Do you prefer a warm color that will make your walls come forward and create a feeling of intimacy? Or do you prefer a cool color that will make your walls recede and give a refreshing feel to your space? How about a neutral room using shades of white, gray, or beige? Or do you prefer a mix of cool and warm colors? Warm schemes often need a touch of a cool hue for balance, and cool schemes need a touch of warmth for stimulation.

ADD DEPTH

The natural beauty of any color is greatly enhanced when you add layers of glaze to your wall. Glaze is untinted paint, or paint with no pigment. To use a glaze, simply stir the paint hue of your choice directly into the glaze. The more or less paint you use, the darker or lighter the effect. The more layers you apply, the richer the color.

The addition of glaze will give a visual depth and translucency to the finished wall. This will allow you to create finishes such as the old world effect of aged walls. For a soft effect, dip a cheesecloth into a glaze mixture, then scrunch the cloth or use a light dabbing motion to apply the glaze to your wall. Use a rolled-up cotton cloth dipped into a tinted glaze to create a loose pattern. Try a sponge dampened in water then dipped in glaze for an edgier effect. Most of the techniques used in this book recommend mixing one part paint with four parts glaze. Remember to mix enough glaze to complete all the walls in your project, because the next batch may not match the color in the first batch. Use a satin or semi-gloss finish to achieve the most depth.

The decorative paint finishes in this book focus on adding color, pattern, texture, or a combination of these to your walls. These basic elements will breathe new life into your rooms. The tools may change as applied to each technique, but the basic principles are still the same. Start by selecting colors that appeal to you and your family and that work for your home. Enhance your wall color by adding pattern and texture for visual interest and excitement.

start with the right tools

A good quality tool can make your paint project go more smoothly. The following tools are used for basic painting and measuring; each is defined to give you an idea of its purpose and use. Look for these tools at your local home center or hardware store. Specialized tools used for decorative painting are shown in the Techniques section starting on page 16.

CAN OPENER Paint cans open easily with this everyday household tool.

COLORED PENCILS Mark measurements and stencil placement with a colored pencil. Select one closest to the paint color you are using. They are easier to use than graphite pencils, which have a tendency to leave smudge marks on the wall.

DROP CLOTHS Protect your floors and furniture with drop cloths before you start any painting project. Plastic is a popular choice; however, it does not absorb spills, and it can be slippery on the floor. Canvas drop cloths both protect and absorb. Look for a heavy cloth with a tight weave for the highest absorbency. Make sure the drop cloth is labeled leak proof or has a rubber backing. With proper care, a canvas cloth will last a long time.

LEVEL Use a carpenter's level to mark accurate horizontal and vertical lines. Levels come in a variety of lengths. There are levels available with printed measurements that allow you to measure and mark at the same time.

LINT-FREE COTTON CLOTHS Keep cloths on hand to clean up spills. White, 100-percent cotton cloths are the best choice. Look for a lint-free cloth that is free of particles. Cotton rags are also used for rubbing on stain and glaze in many decorative paint techniques.

MINI ROLLER COVER AND FRAME These are used to apply paint to tight spots where a standard-size roller can't reach and to paint small areas. The most common size is 4 inches wide.

PAINTER'S TAPE Cover or mask off areas prior to painting with blue painter's tape, a type of masking tape. A low-tack or medium adhesion tape will remove easily from surfaces. Various widths are available, including ½ inch, 1 inch, 1½ inches, and 2 inches. Brown painter's tape works best on smooth walls, creating a nice, crisp line. Apply brown tape with the sticky edge butted into the corner.

PAINTER'S TOOL An indispensable tool for basic painting, this tool will open cans, act as a putty knife, scrape tight areas with a notched end, and remove excess paint from roller covers. The bottom can also be used to pound the lid back onto paint cans.

PAINT TRAY Use a tray to disperse paint onto a roller. A tray generally has a deep end for dipping and a ribbed surface to roll over for distributing the paint evenly onto the roller.

PAINT TRAY LINER Line your paint tray with a disposable plastic liner for easy cleanup. Simply remove it when you are finished painting and throw it away. As an alternative to using a liner, slip your paint tray inside a plastic trash bag.

PLASTIC CONTAINER WITH PREPRINTED MEASUREMENTS Containers with preprinted measurements make it easy to measure glazes. It's also a good idea to keep a container of water on hand for dampening cloths and quick cleanup.

SHORT HANDLED BRUSH A brush with a short handle is used for painting in tight corners where a long-handled brush can't reach.

STANDARD ROLLER COVER AND FRAME Synthetic fiber roller covers are generally recommended when applying latex paint. Roller covers vary in nap length. Use a short nap for smooth surfaces and a thicker nap to cover rough or textured surfaces. A standard size roller is 9 inches wide. The cover slips easily over a frame with a handle. Select a handle with a threaded hole in the base. This will allow you to add an extension for painting ceilings and other high areas.

STIR STICK Use a stir stick for mixing paints and glazes prior to painting. They are generally available at no charge at your local paint store.

TAPE MEASURE This tool for measuring and marking increments both large and small is also used to accurately measure rooms to calculate paint quantity.

TAPERED TRIM BRUSH A 2-inch angled trim brush is perfect for cutting in trim work. The brush is also good for smaller jobs, touch-ups, and places that are hard to reach.

painting basics

When it comes to painting a room, it's all about preparation. You may find that it takes longer to prepare for a painting project than it does to apply a coat of paint to the walls. However, preparation is the key to an attractive finish and promises long-lasting results. Follow the tips below to ensure that your project goes quickly and smoothly.

PREPARING THE ROOM

Preparing a room for painting involves four steps—removing small items, covering up larger items that can't be removed, cleaning the wall surface, and repairing imperfections. To start, relocate smaller items, including those hanging on the walls, to an adjacent room. Move furniture to the center of the room and cover with a drop cloth. A plastic drop cloth works best over furniture because it won't allow paint to soak through. Cover items that you can't remove and aren't planning to paint, such as radiators. Remove electrical switch plates. If you are planning to paint the ceiling, remove the ceiling plates of hanging light fixtures and cover the fixtures. If you prefer, you can paint around the base of the fixtures instead. Finally, cover the floors completely with a drop cloth.

Once everything is out of the way or covered, you are ready to clean the walls of any grease, dirt, or dust that may prevent a new coat of paint from adhering to the surface. Wash the walls with a mixture of household detergent and water. Wipe with a damp cloth and allow to dry. For stubborn areas that require a stronger cleaner, use trisodium phosphate detergent (commonly known as TSP), following the manufacturer's instructions. Protect your hands by wearing rubber gloves and rinse the area with a sponge and water.

Once the surface is clean, remove loose paint with a putty knife and sand the edges until smooth. Remove dust by wiping the surface with a tack cloth. Repair any holes and cracks in the walls, including holes left from artwork that will not be replaced when the project is completed. There are fillers available that are appropriate for each type of wall surface, including new drywall, plaster, and previously painted surfaces. Inquire at your local paint center to find the right filler for your walls. After you select a product, apply by following the manufacturer's instructions.

You will need to prime any new construction or patched areas on the wall. Apply a stain-blocking primer to marks that can't be removed to prevent them from bleeding through the finished coat of paint. Allow to dry completely before applying paint to the walls.

APPLYING PAINT

When you are ready to paint, always paint from top to bottom—start with the ceiling, then move to the walls, and save

HOW MUCH PAINT?

MOST PAINT LABELS STATE ONE GALLON OF PAINT WILL COVER BETWEEN 250 AND 400 SQUARE FEET OF INTERIOR SURFACES. WHEN YOU ARE ESTIMATING PAINT FOR YOUR PROJECT, PLAN ON 300 SQUARE FEET PER GALLON AS AN AVERAGE. BUY ONLY THE AMOUNT OF PAINT YOU NEED FOR YOUR PROJECT, WITH JUST A LITTLE LEFT OVER FOR TOUCHING UP. KEEP IN MIND THAT YOU CAN BUY PAINT IN DIFFERENT QUANTITIES, FROM A QUART TO A GALLON.

FACTS ABOUT SHEEN

LATEX PAINT IS AVAILABLE IN SEVERAL SHEENS: FLAT, SATIN, SEMIGLOSS, AND GLOSS. SOME PAINT MANUFACTURERS CONSIDER SATIN AND EGGSHELL AS THE SAME SHEEN. OTHERS CATEGORIZE EGGSHELL AFTER FLAT WITH JUST A HINT MORE SHINE AND DURABILITY.

■ FLAT PAINT IS THE LEAST REFLECTIVE OF ALL SHEENS, LIMITING THE APPEARANCE OF BLEMISHES AND IMPERFECTIONS ON THE WALL. IT HAS THE LOWEST DURABILITY OF ALL THE SHEENS. IT'S MOST COMMONLY USED IN LOW-ACTIVITY AREAS, SUCH AS FAMILY ROOMS, HALLWAYS, LIVING ROOMS, DINING ROOMS, BEDROOMS, AND ON CEILINGS.

■ SATIN PAINT OFFERS MORE SHINE AND RESISTANCE TO STAINS THAN FLAT PAINT. USE IT IN PLACES THAT REQUIRE MORE CLEANUP, SUCH AS A CHILD'S ROOM. IT'S A POPULAR FINISH FOR OTHER ROOMS AS WELL. IT'S THE IDEAL SHEEN TO USE FOR DECORATIVE PAINTING AND FAUX FINISHING.

■ SEMIGLOSS PAINT IS MORE REFLECTIVE THAN SATIN PAINT. IT'S GENERALLY USED ON WOODWORK TO SET OFF ARCHITECTURAL DETAILS. IT'S AN APPROPRIATE FINISH FOR HALLWAYS, KITCHENS, AND BATHS DUE TO THE SMOOTHER SURFACE THAT ALLOWS FOR EASY CLEANUP. THIS FINISH ACCENTUATES WALL IMPERFECTIONS.

■ GLOSS PAINT HAS THE HIGHEST REFLECTIVE QUALITIES. THIS SHEEN HIGHLIGHTS WALL IMPERFECTIONS MORE THAN ANY OTHER SHEEN. IT'S BEST FOR HIGH-TRAFFIC AREAS ONLY. IT'S MOST GENERALLY USED ON SMALL AREAS, SUCH AS CABINET DOORS OR TRIM. THIS FINISH IS THE MOST DURABLE AND EASIEST TO WASH.

the trim for last. Begin by opening windows and turning on a fan to ventilate the area. Tape off the baseboard and trim with 2-inch painter's tape. Cover light switches and receptacles with tape as well. Slightly dampen your paint brush (or roller) with water and blot onto a paper towel before dipping into paint. The water will help the applicators absorb more paint. To paint the ceiling, use a 2-inch tapered trim brush and paint a 3-inch wide strip to outline the ceiling. This is referred to as "cutting in." Add an extension to the handle of your roller to help you reach the area without a ladder. Evenly coat your roller with paint by dipping it into the deep portion of the paint tray and rolling it over the ridges to remove excess paint. Paint across the width rather than the length of the ceiling. Move the roller back and forth until the ceiling is completed. Allow the ceiling to dry completely before you move to the walls.

Cut in the walls at the ceiling line, in the corners, above the baseboard, and around the window trim and door. Then work with the roller, applying paint in a "W" shape over a 2×2-foot section of the wall. Roll horizontally to spread the paint, then vertically to fill in any unpainted sections. Work on one wall at a time until the room is done. After the first coat is dry, apply a second coat if needed. It's best to apply two thin coats rather than one heavy coat. A heavy coat can dry unevenly and leave lap marks—visible areas where the paint overlaps. If you need a break before the job is completed, wrap your brush (or roller) in plastic wrap to keep the paint from drying.

If you stop for the day, place the wrapped applicators in the freezer until you are ready to resume painting. Take the applicator out of the freezer a couple of hours before you resume painting so the paint has time to thaw.

When you have finished painting, clean and store paint brushes and rollers. Remove as much paint as possible before washing with liquid hand soap and water. Let the water run down the brush to effectively remove the paint from the bristles, while not allowing the paint to get up into the base of the bristles near the handle. Hang brushes to dry. Stand rollers up in the sink to dry. Store in the original plastic sleeve or wrap in aluminum foil.

1

Hold a paint brush as you would a pencil to help reduce hand fatigue. Use a tapered brush when cutting in. Fade the edges to allow the trimmed areas to blend as you apply paint to the rest of the wall.

2

Roll a "W" pattern onto the wall in a 2×2-foot section. Spread the paint out by rolling horizontally and then vertically, filling in unpainted areas.

3

To prevent paint buildup on the rim of the can, use a hammer and nail to punch holes through the rim. This allows excess paint to drain back into the can.

decorative paint techniques

You are about to embark on a process that will change the personality and character of your home. This next section will give you the confidence to try. This section features step-by-step how-to instructions for 50 decorative finishes from basic techniques, such as stripes, faux fabrics, and stenciling, to more challenging techniques, such as aging, plastering, and freehand painting. Skill level is provided with each project on a three-point scale from beginner to intermediate and advanced. Don't be afraid to try a technique that may seem to be beyond your level of experience. You may be surprised at how creative and adept at decorative painting you can be. Practicing first on a sample board until you are comfortable will make all the difference when you finally approach a blank wall.

As you thumb through the techniques, take note of the complete tools list provided with each project; the list includes photographs of specialized tools needed to complete the task. Paint drops help you visualize the colors used in the process. Tips are sprinkled throughout with helpful hints and variations on the technique. Accompanying some of the more popular and versatile techniques are inspirational photographs that show optional colors and designs.

verticalstripes

Striping is an easy painting technique that adds interest to any room and complements any decorating style. Stripes can be created in a variety of widths and color combinations. When you plan your project, let the dimensions of your room be your guide. Bold, wide stripes make small rooms appear larger. Tall, narrow stripes visually raise the ceiling height. One trick to painting stripes is to repaint the base coat color after measuring and taping off stripes. This will prevent the paint from bleeding underneath the tape and create well-defined stripes.

SKILL LEVEL Beginner

TOOLS YOU'LL NEED

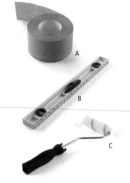

ORANGE SATIN FINISH LATEX PAINT FOR BASE COAT; PINK AND BROWN SATIN FINISH LATEX PAINTS FOR STRIPES

2-INCH LOW-TACK PAINTER'S TAPE (A)

DROP CLOTH

STIR STICKS

PAINT TRAY

STANDARD ROLLER FRAME WITH 9-INCH ROLLER COVER

2-INCH TAPERED TRIM BRUSH

LEVEL WITH PRINTED RULER (B)

COLORED PENCILS IN ORANGE, PINK, AND BROWN

MINI ROLLER FRAME WITH 4-INCH ROLLER COVER (C)

ORANGE, PINK, AND BROWN LATEX PAINTS

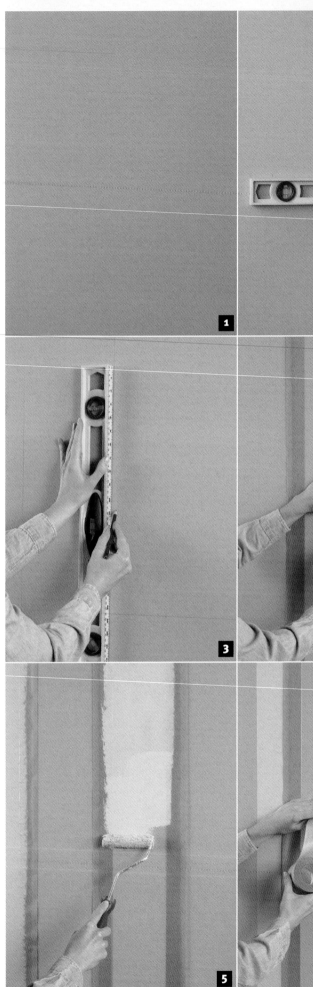

INSTRUCTIONS

Mask ceiling, baseboards, and trim with painter's tape.

1

Paint the entire wall in the orange base color. Paint two coats if necessary. Leave tape on; let dry overnight.

2

Start at the top of the wall and make a series of measurement marks with a colored pencil, moving horizontally across the top. Start measuring opposite the least visible corner and continue around the room. The stripes shown are 8 inches, 5 inches, and 2 inches. Repeat these measurements on all walls.

Allow the stripe to fold around the corner, or adjust your measurements as necessary. If you are striping a room with four walls that join each other, measure the last 4 feet of the wall and adjust the stripe widths to fit the space and continue the pattern.

3

Extend each stripe width vertically with the level, using a colored pencil to draw the lines. Small levels are available to help with tight spaces.

4

Tape all of the 5-inch stripes with painter's tape, pressing down firmly on the inner edges of the tape.

If the wall being painted is textured, you may want to repaint the base coat of the wall color onto the stripe to prevent the paint from bleeding underneath the tape.

5

After the base coat dries, apply the first coat of pink using the mini roller. After the first coat dries, paint a second coat if necessary to ensure a solid stripe.

Remove the tape as soon as the last coat of paint is rolled onto the wall, even if the final coat is still wet.

Allow the paint to dry overnight before taping the 2-inch stripes.

6
Tape the 2-inch stripes using the painter's tape. Press down on the inner edges of the tape.

7
Paint the brown stripe color using the mini roller. Paint a second coat if necessary. Remove all the tape immediately.

8
Allow to dry.

TIPS USE A COLORED PENCIL TO MARK MEASUREMENTS ON THE WALL RATHER THAN A GRAPHITE PENCIL, WHICH IS PRONE TO SMUDGING. USE A COLORED PENCIL THAT MATCHES THE PAINT AND THE MARKS WILL DISAPPEAR.

PLACE A FAN IN THE ROOM TO SPEED DRYING.

verticalstripevariations

1 High-contrast stripes of equal width create an illusion of space in this bathroom because the brown stripes seem closer, while the ivory ones appear to recede.

2 Pairing white with a soft color in equal-width stripes tones down the contrast between dark and light but still offers an impression of depth.

3 For a much more subtle effect, stripe the room in gloss and matte finishes of the same color.

4 Wide low-contrast stripes in soft neutral colors create a formal look in an entry and give the space more importance.

5 Alternating wide and narrow stripes in softly contrasting colors on the top third of the walls in this bathroom play off the geometry of the tiles.

6 In a room full of pattern, medium-width stripes in white plus one color can unify the space by emphasizing the main color.

7 Narrow high-contrast stripes are a good choice for small rooms because they draw the eye upward so the space feels larger.

moiréstripes

Moiré is a shimmering rippling-water effect that you can achieve in paint by moving a combing tool in a smooth "S" pattern from the top to the bottom of your wall. The pattern evokes a sense of movement, but using light-color paint, such as in this lavender-stripe living room, keeps the space feeling tranquil. Combing requires patience and a steady hand. Consider testing the paint and glaze mixture on a primed sample board to ensure the appropriate color and density before tackling a wall. When planning your design, keep in mind that the stripes don't need to match perfectly in width. Some can be a little wider and others narrower.

SKILL LEVEL Intermediate

TOOLS YOU'LL NEED

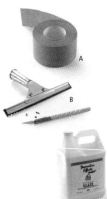

DARK LAVENDER SEMIGLOSS PAINT FOR BASE COAT; PALE LAVENDER SEMIGLOSS PAINT FOR GLAZE COAT

2-INCH LOW-TACK PAINTER'S TAPE (A)

DROP CLOTH

STIR STICKS

PAINT TRAY

LEVEL WITH PRINTED RULER

FINE-TIP MARKER

STANDARD ROLLER FRAME WITH 9-INCH ROLLER COVER

2-INCH TAPERED TRIM BRUSH

SQUEEGEE, 8 INCHES WIDE, AND CRAFTS KNIFE (B)

SELF-HEALING CUTTING MAT

LAVENDER COLORED PENCIL

GLAZE MEDIUM (C)

PLASTIC CONTAINER WITH PRINTED MEASUREMENTS

MINI ROLLER FRAME WITH 4-INCH ROLLER COVER

LINT-FREE COTTON CLOTHS

DARK LAVENDER AND PALE LAVENDER LATEX PAINTS

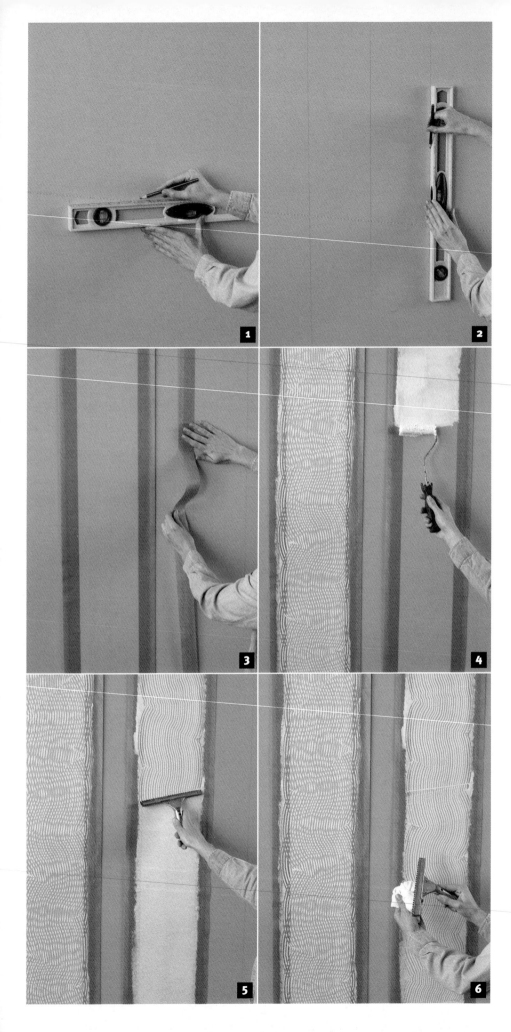

Mask ceiling, baseboards, and trim with painter's tape. Paint the entire wall in the dark lavender base color. Paint two coats if necessary. Leave tape on; let dry overnight.

Use a level with printed ruler and fine-tip marker to mark the blade of the squeegee in ⅛-inch sections. Cut out alternating sections with a crafts knife. Use a safe cutting surface such as a self-healing cutting mat.

1

Measure and mark the stripe widths horizontally every 7 inches, using a colored pencil and level with printed ruler. Measure each wall individually. To avoid having a combed stripe in the corners, which is difficult to execute, plan for a dark lavender stripe to fall in each corner. Adjust the measurements as necessary to work around doors, windows, and other interruptions. Stripes are fine above and below windows, but impossible to comb if the 7-inch stripe falls within a windowsill that juts out, for example.

As you adjust measurements, keep in mind that stripes should not exceed the squeegee width minus 1 inch.

2

Extend the measurements vertically with a level and a colored pencil.

3

Using the painter's tape, tape off every other stripe. Press firmly on the edges of the tape to help keep paint from bleeding underneath.

4

Mix 4 parts glaze to 1 part pale lavender paint in a plastic container. The mixture should roll on easily without dripping. Adjust the glaze-to-paint ratio

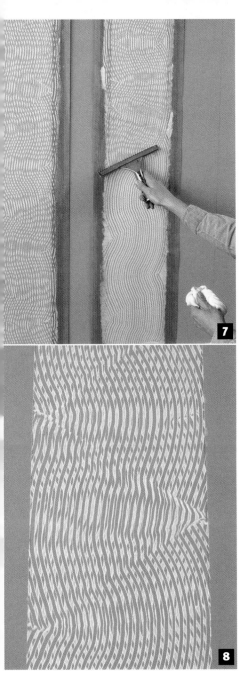

if necessary. With the trim brush, cut in at the ceiling line and baseboards and then roll glaze onto one stripe. Roll a second time over the entire stripe to smooth out the glaze as much as possible.

5

Working quickly from top to bottom, use the squeegee to make a continuous "S" pattern down the length of the stripe. Make sure the squeegee covers the width of the stripe without going beyond the outer edges of the tape.

6

Wipe paint from the squeegee with a cotton cloth.

7

Repeat the "S" pattern from top to bottom, but this time alternate the direction that you started, creating the moiré pattern.

8

Remove tape and repeat with every other stripe until the room or the wall is completed.

Remove all tape; allow to dry overnight.

TIP ADD MORE GLAZE IF THE GLAZE MIXTURE DRIES TOO QUICKLY AND PATCHY AREAS BEGIN TO FORM ON THE WALL, RESISTING COMBING. THIS TECHNIQUE WORKS BEST ON SMOOTH WALLS.

MOIRÉ STRIPE VARIATION USING VARYING-WIDTH STRIPES

MOIRÉ STRIPE VARIATION USING EQUAL-WIDTH STRIPES

horizontal stripes

Turn plain walls into something extraordinary with stripes. Horizontal stripes lead your eye along the wall rather than toward the ceiling, so they can suggest the illusion of greater width or depth. Three tone-on-tone shades create a soft, relaxing atmosphere. The stripes *below* set off the shelving unit, but the design will also work well over a bed or sofa or on one focal-point wall. If you prefer, select contrasting colors to make a bolder statement. But don't hesitate to use different widths of stripes. Sketch your design on paper first to help you visualize your plan before applying paint to the walls.

SKILL LEVEL Beginner

TOOLS YOU'LL NEED

LIGHT BLUE SATIN FINISH LATEX PAINT FOR BASE COAT; MEDIUM AND DARK BLUE SATIN FINISH LATEX PAINTS FOR STRIPES

2-INCH LOW-TACK PAINTER'S TAPE (A)

DROP CLOTH

STIR STICKS

PAINT TRAY

STANDARD ROLLER FRAME WITH 9-INCH ROLLER COVER

2-INCH TAPERED TRIM BRUSH

TAPE MEASURE (B)

BLUE COLORED PENCIL

LEVEL (C)

MINI ROLLER FRAME WITH 4-INCH ROLLER COVER (D)

LIGHT BLUE, MEDIUM BLUE, AND DARK BLUE LATEX PAINTS

INSTRUCTIONS

Mask ceiling, baseboards, and trim with painter's tape. Paint the entire wall in the light blue base color. Paint two coats if necessary. Leave tape on; let dry overnight.

1

Determine the placement of the lowest stripe; mark the bottom edge. (The bottom edge of this lowest stripe is 4 inches above the shelving unit.) Measuring up from this point, mark the wall at increments of 6, 12, 24, 30, and 42 inches.

2

Using a level and colored pencil, mark the first horizontal line all the way around the room. Repeat to draw the remaining horizontal lines.

3

Tape below the bottom line and above the 6-inch line. Repaint the base coat of the wall color onto the stripe to prevent the paint from bleeding underneath the tape. Allow the base coat to dry.

4

Paint the taped-off area with the dark blue; remove tape. Tape below the 12-inch line and above the 24-inch line. Repaint the base coat color; let dry. Paint the taped-off area with the medium blue; remove tape. Tape below the 30-inch line and above the 42-inch line. Repaint the base coat color; let dry. Paint the taped-off area with the dark blue; remove all tape.

5

Allow to dry overnight.

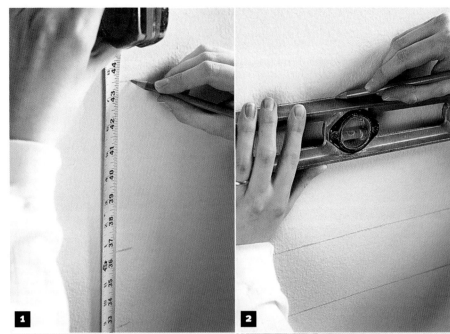

1

2

3

4

5

TIPS CONSIDER ACCESSORIES AS WELL AS LARGER PIECES OF FURNITURE WHEN YOU MAP OUT YOUR DESIGN. THE LAMP AND TABLETOP ACCESSORIES IN THE ROOM OPPOSITE BREAK INTO THE STRIPED AREA, PRESENTING A CAREFULLY PLANNED ARRANGEMENT.

REMOVE THE PAINTER'S TAPE AS SOON AS THE LAST COAT OF PAINT IS ROLLED ONTO THE WALL, EVEN IF THE FINAL COAT IS STILL WET.

horizontalstripevariations

1 Wide light gray and white stripes provide a geometric background for abstract art. The stripes continue on the draperies (although not in the same colors) to help carry the eye around the room.

2 Three bands of color substitute for architectural detailing in this bathroom. Choose three closely related shades to enhance the sense of space.

3 A mirrored wall doubles the impact of equal-width horizontal stripes in a powder room. The high contrast between red and ivory creates a busy look that may be too much for a larger room where you spend a lot of time. In a small guest space, however, the treatment is bold and surprising, adding an element of fun.

4 Wide crisp bands at floor and ceiling levels emphasize the horizontal dimensions of the room, encouraging a relaxed, casual mood. Leaving the largest area free of stripes gives the eye a place to rest so the pattern feels calming rather than busy.

color blocks

Paint an eye-catching, colorful pattern of blocks onto your wall. Select five contrasting colors as shown in the living room *below* for a fun, contemporary setting. If your plan calls for a color-block pattern for an entire room, use subtle colors to suggest an air of serenity. Keep the blocks uniform, even if interrupted by a window or door, to create a sense of movement. When choosing your room's accessories, continue the geometric pattern with square pillows, square picture frames, and cube-shaped vases. Color-block inspiration can come from many sources, such as a favorite item of clothing or bed quilt. For the wall *below*, the color hues were taken from a coffee cup, *opposite top left*.

SKILL LEVEL Beginner

TOOLS YOU'LL NEED

CREAMY TAN SATIN FINISH LATEX PAINT FOR BASE COAT; OLIVE, WHITE, MEDIUM BLUE, AND DARK BLUE SATIN FINISH LATEX PAINTS FOR COLOR BLOCKS

2-INCH LOW-TACK PAINTER'S TAPE (A)

DROP CLOTH

STIR STICKS

PAINT TRAY

STANDARD ROLLER FRAME WITH 9-INCH ROLLER COVER

2-INCH TRIM BRUSH

LEVEL WITH PRINTED RULER (B)

COLORED PENCIL IN BLUE OR TAN

MINI ROLLER FRAME WITH 4-INCH ROLLER COVER (C)

CREAMY TAN, OLIVE, WHITE, MEDIUM BLUE, AND DARK BLUE LATEX PAINTS

INSTRUCTIONS

Mask ceiling, baseboards, and trim with painter's tape. Paint the entire wall in the creamy tan base coat color. Paint two coats if necessary. Leave tape on; let dry overnight.

1

The color blocks shown are 20 inches square. Start the pattern by dividing the wall into 20-inch squares vertically and horizontally. Mark the vertical 20-inch measurements, beginning at the ceiling and ending the pattern at the floor line. If you are blocking the whole room, continue the blocks around the corners, or measure each wall and adjust the block widths accordingly. Keep the height of the blocks the same on every wall, so the block heights match up around the room. For example, in the room shown, the blocks on one wall measured 20×20 inches, and the blocks on another wall were adjusted to measure 20×19 inches.

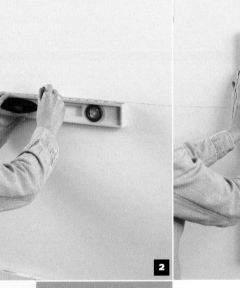

2

Measure the horizontal lines, again making marks as you go.

3

Use a level and colored pencil to draw the vertical and horizontal lines, creating squares across the entire wall. You can use a different colored pencil for each color block to help you visualize the design.

4

Tape off the squares of one color. Press down firmly on tape edges to keep paint from bleeding underneath.

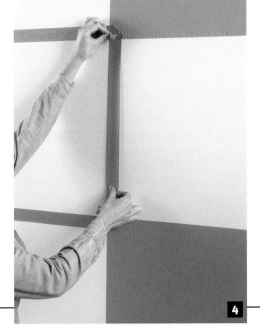

TIP WHEN PLANNING YOUR DESIGN, PAINT SQUARES OF PAPER AND ARRANGE THEM ON A TABLE UNTIL YOU ARE SATISFIED WITH THE OUTCOME OR MAP OUT A DESIGN ON PAPER USING GRAPH PAPER AND A PENCIL.

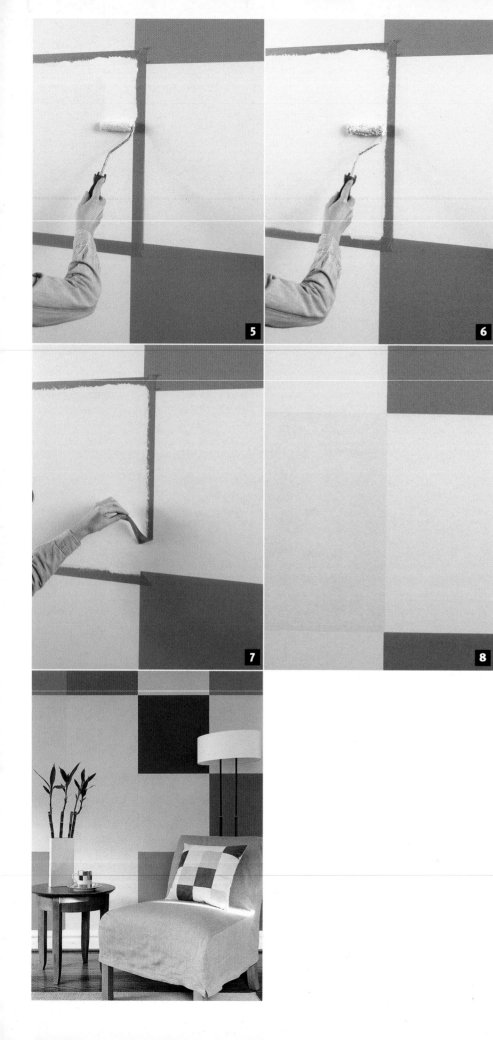

5

Use the mini roller to repaint the base coat color onto the block. This helps prevent the paint from bleeding underneath the tape.

Allow the base coat to dry.

6

Paint one color at a time. Leave some of the blocks in the original base coat color.

7

While the paint is still wet, carefully remove the tape so you don't pull up any paint.

Allow paint to dry.

8

Repeat the taping and painting process with the remaining colors, one color at a time.

Remove all tape; allow to dry.

TIP ADD A BORDER BETWEEN BLOCKS TO CREATE A GRID DESIGN. GRIDS CAN BE CREATED USING TWO OR MORE COLORS. ALLOW FOR A SPACING OF **2** INCHES OR MORE BETWEEN EACH SECTION AND FOR BASEBOARD OR TRIM. TAPE OFF EACH SECTION USING PAINTER'S TAPE. FOR EASY TAPING, MAKE THE BORDER THE WIDTH OF THE TAPE.

colorblockvariations

1 Creating a mosaic of randomly sized blocks requires careful planning on graph paper to figure block dimensions and color placement. Transfer the design to the wall using a level and colored pencils.
2 Enlarge color blocks so that each color fills an entire quadrant of the wall. The colors are all the same value (degree of lightness or darkness) so the effect is spirited and colorful without being visually noisy.
3 Bring high-energy color to a child's room with a grid of blocks in bright colors.

Paint the wall a base color and use wide painter's tape to divide it into blocks. Paint the blocks in the colors of your choice, placing them randomly. When you remove the painter's tape, the base color is revealed as the grid.

metallicblocks

Create the subtle, elegant shimmer of polished silver on your wall using layers of metallic glazes along with thin layers of interference and iridescent colors. This technique uses four basic steps: painting a slate blue base coat, marking and taping the blocks, applying layers of glaze, and adding random highlights of interference (opalescent) and iridescent colors to enhance the metallic effect. Although the process is time-consuming due to the taping, drying, and retaping of the blocks, the final result is worth the effort and will add an intriguing shimmer to your dining room, entryway, or alcove.

SKILL LEVEL Intermediate

TOOLS YOU'LL NEED

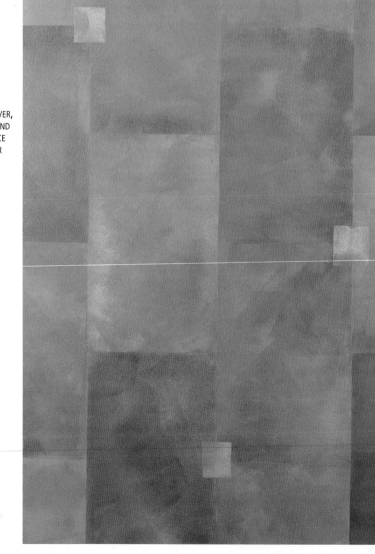

SLATE BLUE LATEX PAINT; SILVER, GOLD, AND BRONZE METAL AND PATINA GLAZES; INTERFERENCE BLUE; AND IRIDESCENT SILVER

SLATE BLUE FLAT FINISH LATEX PAINT FOR BASE COAT; SILVER, GOLD, AND BRONZE METAL AND PATINA GLAZES; INTERFERENCE BLUE AND IRIDESCENT SILVER ACRYLIC PAINTS

1-INCH LOW-TACK PAINTER'S TAPE (A)

DROP CLOTH

STIR STICKS

PAINT TRAY

STANDARD ROLLER FRAME WITH 9-INCH ROLLER COVER

2-INCH TAPERED TRIM BRUSH

METAL YARDSTICK (B)

GRAPHITE PENCIL

3 SMALL DISPOSABLE ALUMINUM PANS (C)

2 SMALL PAINT ROLLERS FOR SMOOTH SURFACES (D)

SCRAP FOAM CORE

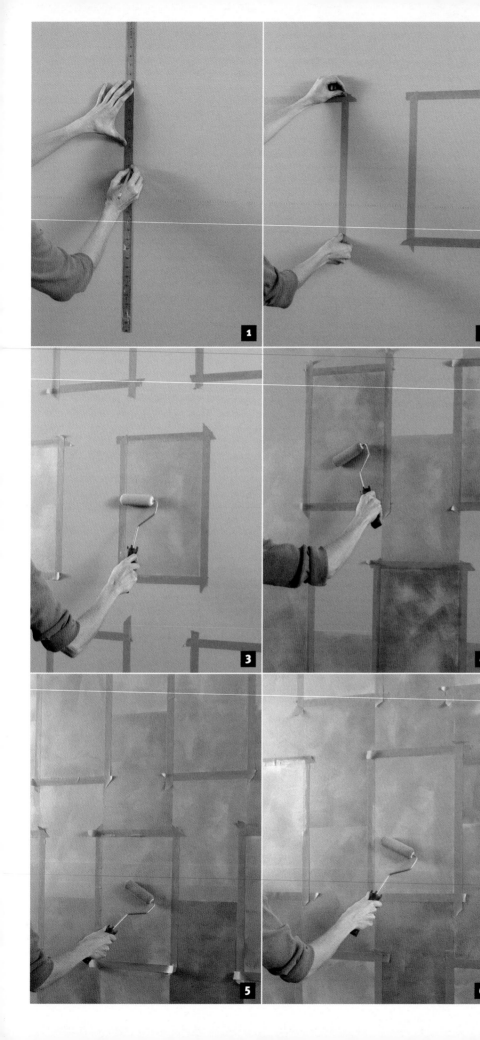

INSTRUCTIONS

Mask ceiling, baseboards, and trim with painter's tape. Paint the entire wall in the slate blue base coat color. Paint two coats if necessary. Leave the tape on; let dry overnight.

1

Use a pencil and yardstick to lightly mark the block design onto the wall.

2

Tape around the outside of several blocks using painter's tape. Our blocks are approximately 10×15 inches.

3

Pour small amounts of silver, gold, and bronze glaze into three small aluminum pans. The metallic blocks shown are painted with different glaze combinations. Some blocks were painted with only one glaze color, while others were painted with two or more glazes. Use a small paint roller to apply a thin layer of glaze to the taped-off blocks. Dip the roller into a pan of glaze and roll it on a scrap of foam before applying to the wall. This allows you to control how evenly the glaze goes onto the surface and eliminates any pattern transfer from the bottom of the pan to the wall. Let the glaze dry.

4

Remove tape and tape off new blocks. Gradually build up layers of glaze, allowing the glaze to dry between coats. Keep the layers light, and vary the pressure with the roller to create different textural effects from block to block. Let dry.

5

Remove tape and tape off remaining blocks. Repeat the process of applying glaze to the blocks. Vary the look by allowing the base coat to show through on some of the blocks and applying heavier layers of glaze on others.

6

After all the blocks are dry, retape selected blocks. Squeeze a small amount of interference blue into a small paint pan and apply a thin layer of color to the edges of the blocks or to entire blocks for highlights. Remove remaining tape; allow to dry.

7

Choose random intersecting corners and tape off a small square approximately 3×3 inches. Roll or brush on iridescent silver. You may need to apply two coats for opacity. Remove remaining tape; allow to dry.

8

After completing the entire wall, step back and evaluate the effect. Add more highlights and sharpen edges as desired.

Allow to dry overnight.

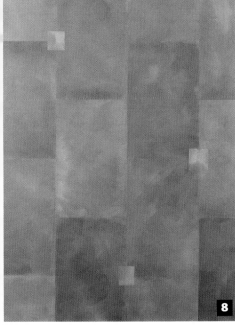

TIPS ALLOW THE BASE COAT TO SHOW THROUGH THE GLAZES.

USE A METAL OR PLASTIC YARDSTICK AS OPPOSED TO A WOODEN ONE TO ENSURE MORE ACCURATE MEASUREMENTS AND STRAIGHTER LINES.

VARY THE FINISH FROM BLOCK TO BLOCK BY PRESSING HARDER AS YOU ROLL THE GLAZE ONTO SELECTED BLOCKS AND APPLYING LIGHTER PRESSURE TO OTHERS.

METALLIC BLOCK BURNISHED GOLD VARIATION IN ANTIQUE WHITE LATEX PAINT; COPPER, GOLD, AND BRONZE METAL AND PATINA GLAZES; AND INTERFERENCE GOLD

METALLIC BLOCK AGED COPPER VARIATION IN MINT GREEN LATEX PAINT; GOLD AND BRONZE METAL AND PATINA GLAZES; AND INTERFERENCE ORANGE

combing

Combing is a fun technique that yields a pinstripe effect when you pull a comb through a wet glaze coat to reveal the base coat color underneath. Select base coat and glaze colors from the same color family for a subtle yet pleasing result. Several types of combing tools are available. A notched squeegee was used for the room shown *below*. The notches in the comb are purposely imperfect, ranging in size from 1/8 inch to 3/8 inch. A prenotched squeegee can be found in the faux finish section of most paint departments. Combing is most effective in small spaces, such as below a chair rail, above wainscoting, or within panels.

SKILL LEVEL Intermediate

TOOLS YOU'LL NEED

DEEP RED SEMIGLOSS LATEX PAINT FOR BASE COAT; PEACH SEMIGLOSS LATEX PAINT FOR GLAZE COAT

2-INCH LOW-TACK PAINTER'S TAPE (A)

DROP CLOTH

STIR STICKS

PAINT TRAY

STANDARD ROLLER FRAME WITH 9-INCH ROLLER COVER (B)

2-INCH TAPERED TRIM BRUSH

PLASTIC CONTAINER WITH PRINTED MEASUREMENTS

GLAZE MEDIUM (C)

RULER

FINE-TIP MARKER

SQUEEGEE AND CRAFTS KNIFE (D)

SELF-HEALING CUTTING MAT

LINT-FREE COTTON CLOTHS

DEEP RED AND PEACH LATEX PAINTS

INSTRUCTIONS

Mask ceiling, baseboards, and trim with painter's tape. Paint the entire wall in the deep red base coat color. Paint two coats if necessary. Leave tape on; let dry overnight. Mix 4 parts glaze to 1 part peach paint in a plastic container. The mixture should roll on easily without dripping. Adjust the glaze to paint ratio if needed. Tape off the corners of adjacent walls to prevent them from accumulating excess glaze. Use a ruler and fine-tip marker to mark the blade of the squeegee in sections varying from ⅛ inch to ⅜ inch. Cut out alternating sections with a crafts knife. Use a safe cutting surface such as a self-healing cutting mat.

1

Start in the corner and move toward the center of the wall, trimming and rolling the glaze onto the wall vertically and working in an approximately 4-foot-wide section.

2

Hold the squeegee firmly and carefully drag it down the just-glazed wall in one continuous motion. Continue combing down the wall, using the just-combed section as a guide.

3

Wipe the squeegee as necessary with a damp cloth.

4 5

Repeat the process, alternating between rolling glaze and combing, until the entire wall is completed. Completely finish one wall at a time without stopping. Remove the tape before the glaze dries. Allow finished walls to dry before combing adjoining ones. Remove remaining tape when completed.

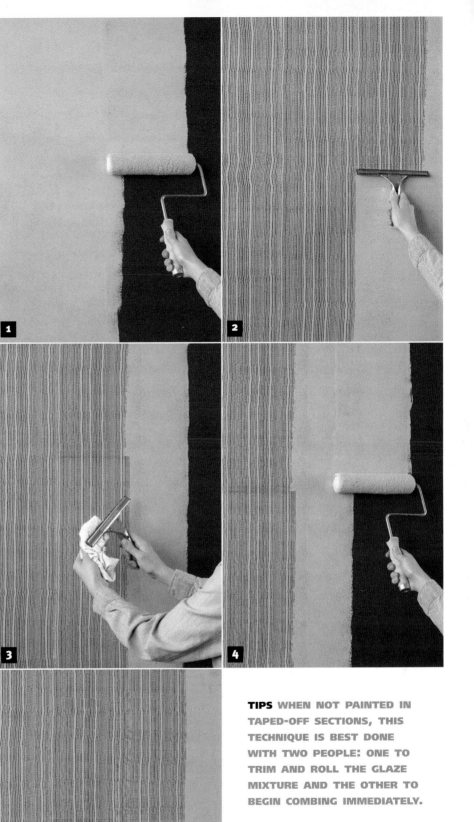

TIPS WHEN NOT PAINTED IN TAPED-OFF SECTIONS, THIS TECHNIQUE IS BEST DONE WITH TWO PEOPLE: ONE TO TRIM AND ROLL THE GLAZE MIXTURE AND THE OTHER TO BEGIN COMBING IMMEDIATELY.

WHEN COMBING INTO AN AREA NARROWER THAN THE COMBING TOOL SUCH AS A CORNER, USE A SMALL BRUSH TO PAINT BACK SLIGHTLY INTO THE AREA ALREADY COMBED TO ACCOMMODATE THE WIDTH OF THE COMB.

7

harlequindiamonds

Always in motion, the harlequin diamond pattern brings a sense of playfulness and fun to any room's decor. Painted in neutral colors, diamonds provide a clean, sophisticated appearance. Painted in bright contrasting colors, they add energy to a room. When planning your pattern, keep the size of your room and furnishings in mind. Measure the wall height and length, then divide each measurement by the number of diamonds you would like. Keep dividing until you find a measurement that works for your wall size. The smaller the pattern, the more labor-intensive the process because you will need to measure, mark, and paint more diamonds. Consider this technique for a focal-point wall rather than an entire room, and paint adjoining walls in one of the colors.

SKILL LEVEL Advanced

TOOLS YOU'LL NEED

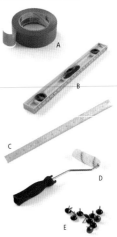

LIGHT LIME GREEN SATIN FINISH LATEX PAINT FOR BASE COAT; DARK LIME GREEN SATIN FINISH LATEX PAINT FOR DIAMONDS

2-INCH LOW-TACK PAINTER'S TAPE (A)

DROP CLOTH

STIR STICKS

PAINT TRAY

STANDARD ROLLER FRAME WITH 9-INCH ROLLER COVER

2-INCH TAPERED TRIM BRUSH

LEVEL WITH PRINTED RULER (B)

GREEN COLORED PENCIL

METAL YARDSTICK (C)

MINI ROLLER FRAME WITH 4-INCH ROLLER COVER (D)

BLACK UPHOLSTERY TACKS (E)

BLACK SPRAY PAINT, OPTIONAL

HAMMER

DRY CLOTH

LIGHT LIME GREEN AND DARK LIME GREEN LATEX PAINTS

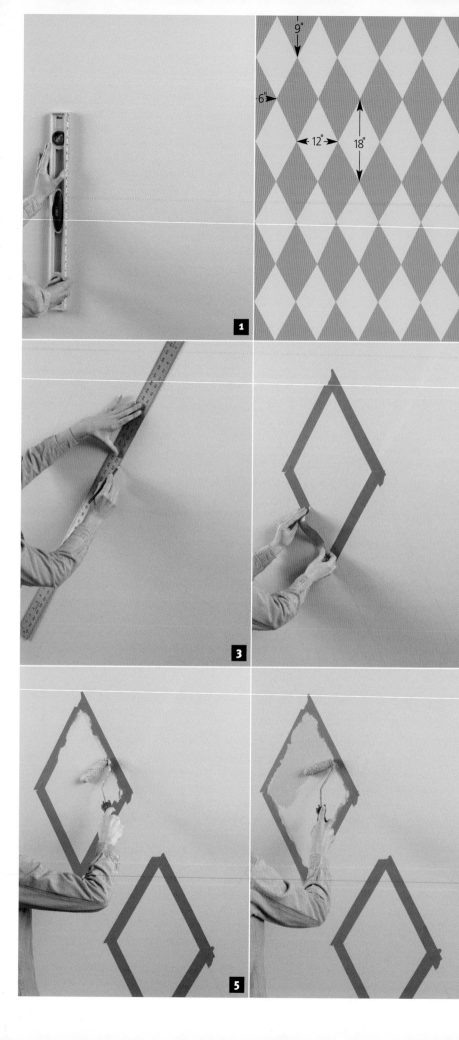

Mask ceiling, baseboards, and trim with painter's tape. Paint the entire wall in the light lime green base coat color. Paint two coats if necessary. Leave tape on; let dry overnight.

1

Decide on the height and width of the diamond pattern. The diamonds shown are 12 inches wide and 18 inches tall. If you are extending the diamond pattern around the whole room, keep the height of the diamonds the same on every wall. Adjust the width as necessary to fit the wall length. Take the time to work this out on paper. A sketch can help you picture the scale and placement of the diamond pattern so you know where and how to begin marking your measurements.

2

Working on one wall at a time, use a level with printed measurements to find and mark all the diamond points. Measure vertically and horizontally using half-diamond widths and heights staggered as shown in the diagram in Photo 2. Each diamond has four points and is connected to the next diamond.

3

Connect the dots with a straight-edge. You can skip this step if you prefer and just tape off the diamonds by using the dots that you measured as your guide. Place a small piece of tape on the diamonds you don't want to paint to help distinguish them from the diamonds that you do want to paint.

4

Tape off every other diamond to be painted. Remember to skip around since the tape doesn't allow you to paint every other diamond at the same time. Tape off as many diamonds as you can.

5

Repaint the base coat color to prevent the paint from bleeding underneath the tape. Allow to dry.

6

Paint the taped-off diamonds in the dark lime green color by using a mini roller. Allow to dry.

7

Continue taping off and painting diamonds. Remove the tape as you finish painting. Remove remaining tape; allow to dry.

8

Spray tacks with black spray paint if black upholstery tacks are not available. Allow to dry.

Pound the tacks into the diamond points. Put a piece of dry cloth or felt over the tack to prevent it from being scratched by the hammer. Use a rubber mallet if desired.

TIP IT CAN BE VERY DIFFICULT TO DRAW LINES AND HOLD A LEVEL AT THE SAME TIME. TRY PLACING A SMALL PIECE OF ROLLED TAPE, STICKY SIDE OUT, ONTO EACH END OF THE STRAIGHTEDGE. PUT THE LEVEL IN PLACE AND DRAW THE LINE.

harlequindiamondvariations

1 A palette of taupe, cream, and black offers a neutral color scheme for a harlequin diamond wall and checkerboard floor in this bright and airy bath.

2 A harlequin paint finish in tones of caramel and camel replaces a fireplace surround in this living room.

3 Diamond patterns aren't limited to the wall. Green and white diamonds enhance the floor of this porch. Polyurethane gives the finish durability.

4 Seven hues of green diamonds provide a focal point in this living room.

The surrounding walls are color-washed in soft green.

5 A subtle diamond pattern in warm yellow balances the bright colors and patterns in this child's room.

6 Chalk lines were snapped across the wall to outline these 2×3-foot diamonds. The chalk lines provide a painterly effect with uneven edges.

7 The color-washed diamonds in this baby's room were created using two shades of the same color, one thinned to a translucent shade.

polkadots

Paint a roomful of playful polka dots using a simple handmade stencil. The dots in the room *opposite* are painted with pure white using a swirling circular motion that gives each one a color-washed effect. The polka dots are 5 inches in diameter and are staggered 18 inches apart. Like other techniques featuring geometric shapes, this one requires careful measuring. The pink-and-white pattern shown is perfect for a child's bedroom, but if painted in other contrasting or tone-on-tone colors, this design could easily fit into a lighthearted kitchen, dining room, or bath.

SKILL LEVEL Intermediate

TOOLS YOU'LL NEED

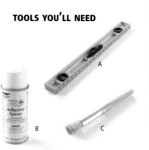

PINK SATIN FINISH LATEX PAINT FOR BASE COAT; WHITE SATIN FINISH LATEX PAINT FOR POLKA DOTS

2-INCH LOW-TACK PAINTER'S TAPE

DROP CLOTH

STIR STICKS

PAINT TRAY

STANDARD ROLLER FRAME WITH 9-INCH ROLLER COVER

2-INCH TAPERED TRIM BRUSH

PENCIL

PAPER

LEVEL WITH PRINTED RULER (A)

COLORED PENCIL

ROUND BOWL OR OTHER ITEM TO TRACE, APPROXIMATELY 5 INCHES IN DIAMETER

INK PEN

STENCIL PLASTIC

CRAFTS KNIFE

SELF-HEALING CUTTING MAT

STENCIL SPRAY ADHESIVE (B)

FOAM PLATE

LARGE STENCIL BRUSH (C)

PINK AND WHITE LATEX PAINTS

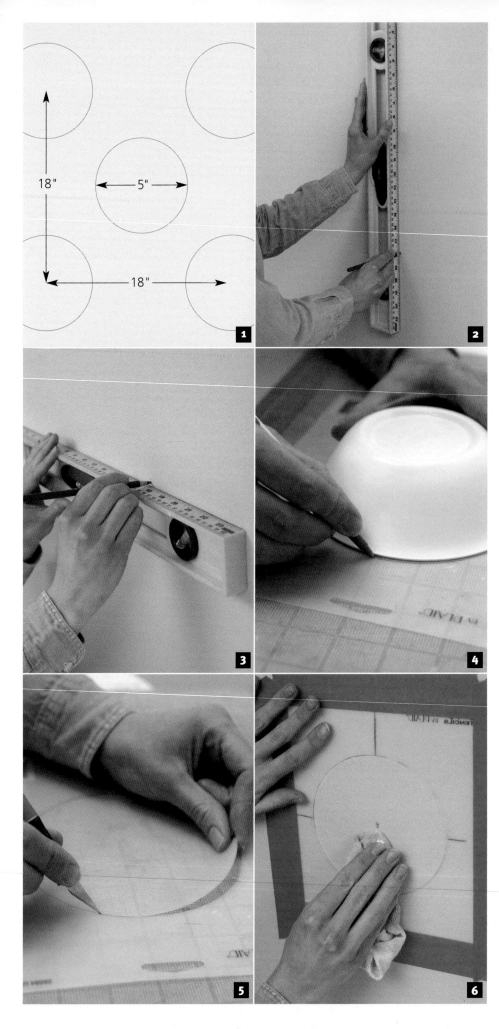

Mask ceiling, baseboards, and trim with painter's tape. Paint the entire wall in the pink base coat color. Paint two coats if necessary. Leave tape on; let dry overnight.

1

Decide on the height and width of the polka-dot pattern. The polka dots shown are 5 inches in diameter and are staggered vertically and horizontally 18 inches apart from the center of each polka dot as shown in the diagram. Measure the height and width of each wall. If you are extending the polka-dot pattern around the whole room, keep the height of the polka dots the same on every wall. Adjust the width between them as necessary to fit the wall length.

For example, divide the wall width by 18 inches and see where you come out. Adjust the width spacing, staying as close to 18 inches, or your pattern width, as possible. The polka dots on two of the walls in the room shown are spaced 18 inches in height and 17 inches in width. The other two are spaced 18 inches in height and $17\frac{3}{8}$ inches in width. This allows the pattern to line up completely around the room on each wall, starting and ending with a half polka dot on the ceiling line, corners, and baseboard.

Take the time to work this out on paper. A sketch can help you picture the scale and placement of the polka dot pattern so you know where and how to begin marking your measurements.

2

Using a level, begin marking the pattern onto the wall, one wall at a time. Measure along the ceiling line first, then down the wall on each side, making small marks with a colored pencil to indicate the center of each polka dot. This will be the first row of polka dots, starting with a half polka dot.

The first one will be 9 inches from the corner of the adjoining wall.

3

Because the pattern is staggered, the next row will be the full 18 inches in from the corner of the adjoining wall and approximately 9 inches down from the first row as shown in the diagram.

Continue marking the center of each polka dot until one wall is completed. Stand back from the wall from time to time to check your work. This will allow you to catch mistakes before the whole wall is finished. Mark all the walls you wish to paint.

4

Using an ink pen, trace a bowl or cup of the appropriate size onto a piece of stencil plastic. Draw a vertical and horizontal line to divide the circle into quarters, extending the lines beyond the circle as well. These lines will help you center the stencil on the small dots on the wall.

5

Cut out the circle carefully using a crafts knife with a new blade. Use a safe cutting surface, such as a self-healing cutting mat.

Spray the back of the stencil with spray adhesive. Add painter's tape if desired.

6

Align the stencil with the small dot on the wall in the middle of the stencil. Use the vertical and horizontal lines to help you visually center the small dot inside the stencil. Wipe off the small dot if it will show through the white paint.

7

Place a small amount of white paint onto a foam plate. Dip the stencil brush in the white paint and stencil the polka dot, brushing in a swirling, circular motion. This will give the polka dots a circular, washy feel. The polka dots shown are not painted solid white.

8

Brush from the stencil toward the center of the polka dot to keep the paint from bleeding under the edge of the stencil. If bleeding occurs, use less paint on the stencil brush and swirl the edges of the polka dot.

Continue stenciling polka dots until you are finished with the whole ones. Then, cut the stencil in half and stencil the half polka dots using the same swirling, circular technique.

Remove remaining tape; allow to dry.

TIP IF YOU DON'T HAVE A FOAM PLATE, USE THE LID FROM A QUART CAN OF WHITE PAINT. SHAKE THE CAN, THEN TAKE THE LID OFF AND TURN IT PAINT-SIDE UP. IT'S JUST THE RIGHT AMOUNT OF PAINT FOR STENCILING. BLOT EXCESS PAINT OFF YOUR BRUSH ONTO A PAPER TOWEL BEFORE STENCILING.

denimfinish

Give your walls the worn fabric look of an old denim shirt. A faux-denim wall finish can give a casual, relaxed appearance to any room. The denim effect uses two specially designed tools: a denim weaver brush and denim check roller. The denim weaver brush creates a crosshatch pattern when dragged through a wet glaze mixture that has been applied to the wall. A denim check roller, which has notched metal disks, creates the worn fabric appearance when rolled over the glazed surface. The process must be done quickly before the glaze begins to dry. Light blue and medium blue hues are most common for this technique. But the effect can look equally impressive in other colors, such as red. Try this technique in any room where you'd like to add a casual touch, such as a child's bedroom or a family room.

SKILL LEVEL Intermediate

TOOLS YOU'LL NEED

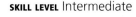

PALE BLUE SEMIGLOSS FINISH PAINT FOR BASE COAT; DARK BLUE SEMIGLOSS FINISH LATEX PAINT FOR GLAZE COAT

2-INCH LOW-TACK PAINTER'S TAPE

DROP CLOTH

STIR STICKS

PAINT TRAY

STANDARD ROLLER FRAME WITH 9-INCH ROLLER COVER

2-INCH TAPERED TRIM BRUSH

LEVEL WITH PRINTED RULER (A)

BLUE COLORED PENCIL

GLAZE MEDIUM (B)

PLASTIC CONTAINER WITH PRINTED MEASUREMENTS

DENIM WEAVER BRUSH (C)

LINT-FREE COTTON CLOTHS

DENIM CHECK ROLLER (D)

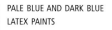

PALE BLUE AND DARK BLUE LATEX PAINTS

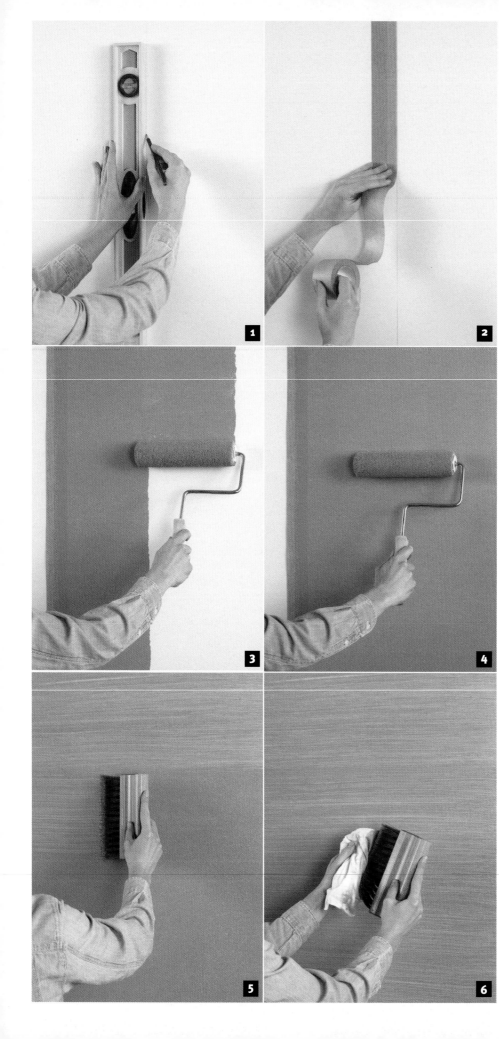

INSTRUCTIONS

Mask ceiling, baseboards, and trim with painter's tape. Paint the entire wall in the pale blue base coat color. Paint two coats if necessary. Leave tape on; let dry overnight.

Divide the room into a series of vertical panels. The panels should be narrow enough that you can work quickly from top to bottom—a width between 18 and 36 inches is generally manageable. For simplicity, choose a width that divides evenly into the width of your wall. The lines where panels meet will resemble seams, so you can divide the wall into horizontal panels if you prefer.

1
Mark off the panels by drawing vertical lines with the level and colored pencil.

2
Tape off alternating sections with the painter's tape.

In a plastic container with preprinted measurements, mix 4 parts glaze to 1 part dark blue paint. Adjust the glaze mixture if necessary. If the mixture is drying too quickly on the wall, add more glaze or see the tip *opposite*.

3
Trim and roll glaze onto the first taped-off section.

4
Quickly roll through the glaze a second time to ensure an even coating.

5
Drag the weaver brush through the glaze horizontally.

6
Wipe the brush with a damp cloth after each stroke.

7

Drag the brush through the glaze vertically, again wiping on a damp cloth after each stroke.

8

Run the check roller horizontally over the brushed section, applying firm pressure.

9

Run the check roller vertically through the same section. Create as much or as little pattern as you desire. Complete the entire panel. Remove the tape.

10

Move on to the next panel, tape it off, and repeat Steps 3–9, removing tape when you are done. Repeat the process for every taped-off panel. Remove all tape and allow to dry.

TIPS IF THE GLAZE MIXTURE IS DRYING TOO QUICKLY, ADD MORE GLAZE, SMALL AMOUNTS OF WATER, PAINT CONDITIONER, OR EVEN A LITTLE DISH SOAP, AND USE THE BRUSH TO REAPPLY ONTO THE WALL. THIS WILL ALLOW THE GLAZE MIXTURE TO SPREAD EASILY.

IF THE TEXTURED SURFACE CREATED BY THE CHECK ROLLER IS DISAPPEARING, WAIT ABOUT ONE MINUTE AND ROLL OVER THE AREA AGAIN. SOMETIMES THE GLAZE IS TOO WET TO HOLD THE ADDED TEXTURE.

WHEN WORKING IN A CORNER, DRAG IN ONE DIRECTION FROM THE CORNER OUTWARD.

denimfinishvariations

1 For a more realistic effect, "seams" have been emphasized in the cobalt blue denim walls in this bath. For seams, section the walls in long vertical panels and overlap the painted edges slightly to create a dark vertical line.

2 A dark blue faux-denim wall provides the perfect backdrop for this denim curtain panel. The use of denim adds a simple, casual touch.

3 Try the faux-denim treatment with colors other than traditional blue. Red glaze over an ivory or tan base coat creates the effect of coarsely woven denim.

4 The highly textured walls in this dining room emphasize the worn look of denim fabric. A coarse short-bristled brush was used in place of the denim check roller and repeatedly dragged horizontally and vertically through wet glaze for a rougher look. The walls complement the country furnishings and accessories.

linenfinish

Give your walls the airy weave of a natural linen fabric. For this look, apply the top coat of glaze mixture using a low-nap roller to ensure a smooth, even coat. While the glaze is still wet, drag a linen weaver brush horizontally and then vertically through the mixture. The brush will remove some of the top glaze coat, allowing a woven pattern to emerge. Small nubs of paint will also appear, giving the walls an authentic linen appearance. Remember to wipe the excess glaze off the brush with each pass for clean strokes. This versatile effect will work in both elegant and casual rooms.

SKILL LEVEL Intermediate

TOOLS YOU'LL NEED

OFF-WHITE SATIN FINISH LATEX PAINT FOR BASE COAT; YELLOW-GOLD SATIN FINISH LATEX PAINT FOR GLAZE COAT

2-INCH LOW-TACK PAINTER'S TAPE (A)

DROP CLOTH

STIR STICKS

PAINT TRAY

STANDARD ROLLER FRAME WITH ¼-INCH NAP PAINT ROLLER COVER

2-INCH TAPERED TRIM BRUSH

LEVEL WITH PRINTED RULER (B)

PENCIL

GLAZE MEDIUM (C)

PLASTIC CONTAINER WITH PRINTED MEASUREMENTS

7-INCH LINEN WEAVER BRUSH (D)

LINT-FREE COTTON CLOTHS

OFF-WHITE AND YELLOW-GOLD LATEX PAINTS

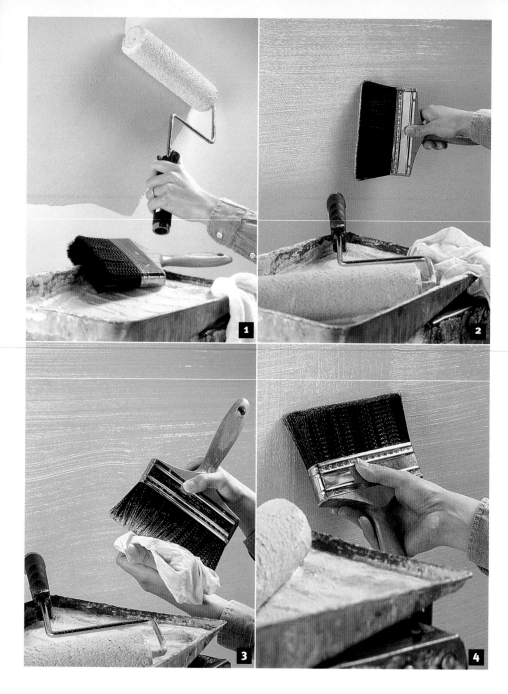

INSTRUCTIONS

Mask ceiling, baseboards, and trim with painter's tape.

1

Paint the entire wall in the off-white base coat color. Paint two coats if necessary. Leave tape on; let dry overnight.

Divide the room into vertical sections about 40 inches wide. Tape the outside edges of every other section with painter's tape. If you end a section in a corner, tape the edge of the adjoining wall where it meets the corner.

Mix 4 parts glaze to 1 part yellow-gold paint in a plastic container. Use a paint roller to apply a thin layer of glaze over an entire taped-off wall section. Finish with light ceiling-to-floor strokes to even out the roller marks.

2

Beginning at the top left-hand corner of the section, drag the dry linen weaver brush across the section from left to right in a smooth, firm stroke. Continue until the section is completed.

3

Wipe the brush with a lint-free cloth after each stroke to remove excess glaze.

4

Drag the brush vertically down the section, working from top to bottom until the panel is finished. Use a light touch on the brush.

Remove the vertical strips of painter's tape immediately after dragging and while the glaze is still wet. Allow the first glazed sections to dry overnight before taping and painting alternate sections. To abut the seams, place the tape on top of the dried glaze along the edge where the sections meet. After all the sections are dry, remove remaining tape.

linenfinishvariations

1

1 Chocolate brown linen walls make a dramatic decorating statement in this dining room. Crisp white on the woodwork and ceiling balance the brown for a mood of understated elegance.

2 The walls in this bath are crosshatched in two shades of blue-purple. White woodwork and accessories enhance the fresh, cool look. Blue-and-white striped fabric brings the wall color into the room, and touches of gold in the mirror and chair add a warm accent.

3 A crosshatched linen pattern adds dressy texture to the apple-green walls in this traditional bedroom. Luxurious fabrics and a diamond-pattern bed canopy add to the striking design.

2 **3**

burlapfinish

This technique replicates the coarse, textured look of burlap fabric. The texturing is created with two squeegees, one notched in smaller sections than the other. Begin the process by applying a dark base coat color. After the base coat dries, apply a light-color glaze mixture evenly on the wall. While the mixture is wet, a squeegee is pulled vertically down the wall, creating stripes. After the first layer of glaze has dried, glaze is then reapplied over the stripes, and a second squeegee is pulled horizontally across, creating a textured basket-weave pattern. A steady hand is required when moving through the glaze. It's best to work in taped-off panels, especially when working alone. It's also important to move quickly before the glaze begins to dry. Golden brown hues, most often associated with burlap fabric, are common colors for this technique. Other neutral shades will also work. Use lighter tones over darker ones.

SKILL LEVEL Intermediate

TOOLS YOU'LL NEED

GOLDEN BROWN SEMIGLOSS FINISH LATEX PAINT FOR BASE COAT; LIGHT TAN SEMIGLOSS FINISH LATEX PAINT FOR GLAZE COAT

2-INCH LOW-TACK PAINTER'S TAPE

DROP CLOTH

STIR STICKS

PAINT TRAY

STANDARD ROLLER FRAME WITH 9-INCH ROLLER COVER

2-INCH TAPERED TRIM BRUSH

RULER

FINE-TIP MARKER

2 SQUEEGEES, LARGE AND SMALL (A)

CRAFTS KNIFE (B)

SELF-HEALING CUTTING MAT

LEVEL WITH PRINTED RULER

TAN COLORED PENCIL

GLAZE MEDIUM (C)

PLASTIC CONTAINER WITH PRINTED MEASUREMENTS

LINT-FREE COTTON CLOTHS

GOLDEN BROWN AND LIGHT TAN LATEX PAINTS

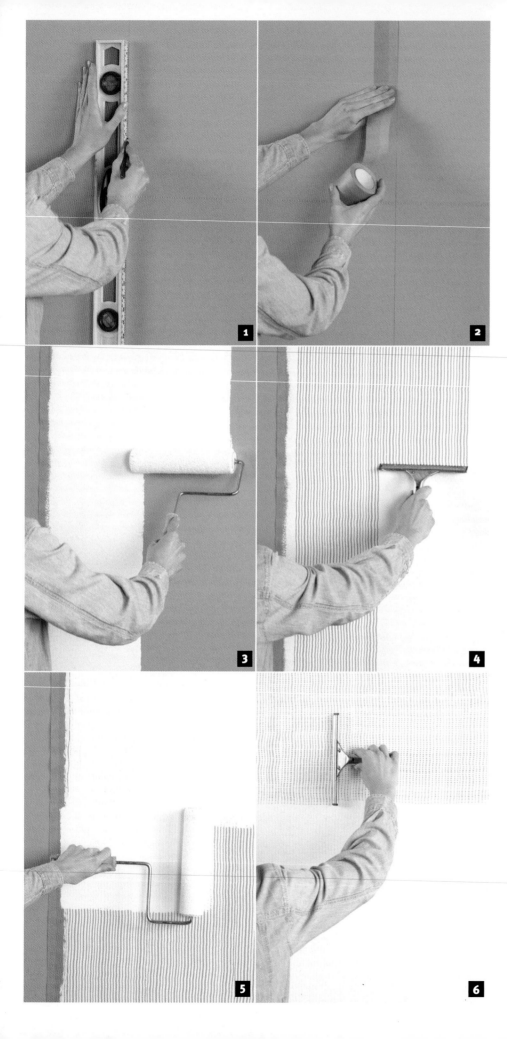

INSTRUCTIONS

Mask ceiling, baseboards, and trim with painter's tape. Paint the entire wall in the golden brown base coat color. Paint two coats if necessary. Leave tape on; let dry overnight.

Use a ruler and fine-tip marker to divide the blade of the large squeegee into ⅛-inch sections. Working on a safe cutting surface, such as a self-healing cutting mat, cut out every other section with a crafts knife. A little variance in the notches is acceptable. Repeat the process on the small squeegee, making the sections 1/16 inch wide or as small as possible.

1

Using a level and colored pencil, draw vertical lines to divide the wall into sections or panels. The wall sections here are 36 inches wide. You may need to adjust the width of the panels to suit the size of your room. Narrower panels may be easier to manage if you are working alone.

2

Tape off alternating panels with painter's tape, pressing down hard on the tape to prevent the paint from bleeding underneath.

Mix 4 parts glaze with 1 part light tan paint in a plastic container.

3

Roll glaze onto the first taped-off panel. Smooth the glaze a second time with the roller to create an even surface.

4

Starting at the top of the glazed section, pull the large squeegee down the wall in one continuous motion to make vertical stripes. Try to complete one run without stopping. If you must stop, begin again slowly. Minimal flaws are acceptable. Use a cloth to wipe excess glaze from the squeegee

as needed. Continue combing vertically across the glazed section using the edge of the previous stroke as a guide until the entire panel is finished.

Repeat the process for each taped off panel. Leave the tape in place and allow to dry completely.

5
Roll the glaze mixture over the section, covering the vertical striping.

6
Starting at the top of the panel, pull the smaller squeegee horizontally through the glaze.

Repeat combing horizontally, working down the wall quickly, until the panel is finished.

7
Wipe excess glaze from the squeegee as needed.

8
Repeat Steps 3–7 until all the taped-off panels are finished. Remove tape after the glaze has dried completely.

Tape off unpainted panels and repeat using the same process. Remove remaining tape; let dry.

TIP WHEN COMBING THROUGH THE GLAZE, START SLOWLY AND KEEP A LIGHT BUT FIRM PRESSURE ON THE SQUEEGEE. GLAZE IS SLIPPERY, AND IF THE PRESSURE ON THE COMB IS TOO FIRM, THE COMB WILL SLIDE AROUND. IF THIS HAPPENS, REROLL THE GLAZE AND START THE PANEL AGAIN.

leatherfinish

Create the luxurious look of leather on your walls. The pattern and texture are created by pressing plastic to the wall with your hands. It's important to work in small, taped-off sections that are easy to manage alone. To vary the leather look in each section, apply the plastic differently in each one—bunch the plastic in one area and simply add dips and curves in others. In selecting a room for this technique, choose one with few doorways and windows. For the most convincing results, use a light background color with a dark glaze on top. In the living area shown *opposite*, a light tan base coat with a warm caramel glaze coat was used.

SKILL LEVEL Intermediate

TOOLS YOU'LL NEED

OFF-WHITE SATIN FINISH LATEX PAINT FOR BASE COAT; WARM CARAMEL SATIN FINISH LATEX PAINT FOR GLAZE COAT

2-INCH LOW-TACK PAINTER'S TAPE (A)

DROP CLOTH

STIR STICKS

PAINT TRAY

STANDARD ROLLER FRAME WITH 9-INCH ROLLER COVER

2-INCH TAPERED TRIM BRUSH

PENCIL

PAPER

TAPE MEASURE

LEVEL (B)

TAN COLORED PENCIL

SCISSORS

PLASTIC DROP CLOTH, 1 MILLIMETER THICK (C)

GLAZE MEDIUM (D)

LINT-FREE COTTON CLOTHS

OFF-WHITE AND WARM CARAMEL LATEX PAINTS

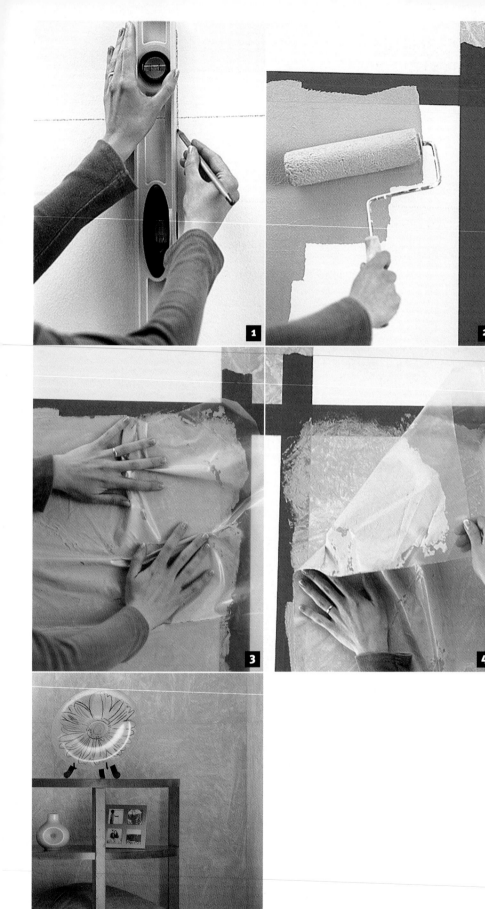

INSTRUCTIONS

Mask ceiling, baseboards, and trim with painter's tape. Paint the entire wall in the off-white base coat color. Paint two coats if necessary. Leave tape on; let dry overnight. Remove ceiling tape.

Measure the height and width of each wall. Draw a small sketch on paper to help you visualize how the rectangular panels should be arranged on the wall. Plan sections that you can manage alone, such as 24- to 48-inch-wide rectangles.

1

Use a tape measure, level, and colored pencil to draw the rectangles on the wall. For each panel, use scissors to cut a piece of plastic drop cloth about a foot longer and wider than the rectangle; set aside. Make a glaze mixture of 4 parts glaze to 1 part warm caramel paint. For the wall on page 65, 1 gallon of glaze was mixed with 1 quart of paint. Tape off every other rectangle; do not tape off the ceiling, because glaze will bleed underneath the tape and dry on the ceiling.

2

Working on one rectangle at a time, roll on the glaze. In the rectangles along the ceiling and baseboard, cut in the glaze mixture along the trim and roll it on over the remainder of the rectangle.

3

Apply plastic to the glazed section. Shape and form as desired, pressing flat with the palms of your hands. Avoid dragging your fingers because lines will appear. Leaving some fingerprints is desirable.

4

Peel the plastic off, starting at one top corner. Remove tape immediately after removing plastic. If glaze has seeped under tape, remove it with a wet cloth; also wipe any excess glaze off woodwork. Allow to dry.

leatherfinishvariations

1 Subtle rectangular shapes highlight the leather treatment in this living room. Working in smaller taped-off sections allows you to vary the design from panel to panel for a more interesting effect.
2 Butter yellow faux-leather walls provide a warm background for wrought-iron panels and wicker chairs.
3 A dark leather sofa complements a faux-leather wall treatment. Because the leather technique works on any smooth, flat surface, try it on tabletops, drawer fronts, and chests. Add embellishments such as upholstery tacks to drive home the illusion of an upholstered leather finish.

suedefabric

Faux-suede walls provide a rich backdrop in a room that begs for a casual style. You can create the velvety look of soft suede by using a specially formulated suede paint. Generally, one color of paint is used to create a suede finish. Two colors of suede paint were used to create the effect in the den *below*. A simple crisscross motion blends the colors, giving the walls a realistic appearance with more nap and texture than the single color provides.

SKILL LEVEL Beginner

TOOLS YOU'LL NEED

SUEDE PAINTS IN MOSS GREEN
AND DARK HUNTER GREEN

2-INCH LOW-TACK
PAINTER'S TAPE

DROP CLOTH

STIR STICKS

PAINT TRAY

2-INCH TAPERED TRIM BRUSH

LEVEL WITH PRINTED RULER(A)

4-INCH SPECIALIZED
SUEDE ROLLER (B)

9-INCH SPECIALIZED
SUEDE ROLLER (C)

3-INCH LATEX PAINTBRUSH (D)

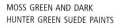

MOSS GREEN AND DARK
HUNTER GREEN SUEDE PAINTS

INSTRUCTIONS

Mask ceiling, baseboards, and trim with painter's tape.

1

Using the dark hunter green, trim the corners and ceiling lines in a 28-inch section or three roller cover widths. Roll the 4-inch suede roller vertically from floor to ceiling, filling in the trimmed area. Try not to roll through paint that has dried.

2

Roll over the 28-inch painted section with the 9-inch suede roller to smooth out the paint. Continue working in 28-inch-wide sections, trimming, rolling on wet paint with the 4-inch roller, and smoothing out the paint with the 9-inch roller until the entire wall is finished.

This coat of paint will look uneven. Allow to dry.

3

Dip the 3-inch latex paintbrush alternately into the moss green and dark hunter green paints and brush in random X strokes after each dip. Continue the crisscross pattern, blending the light and dark colors. Trim in the corners but drag the brush in the X pattern to avoid straight lines in the corners.

4

Continue working in the same manner until the entire wall is finished. Remove tape; allow to dry.

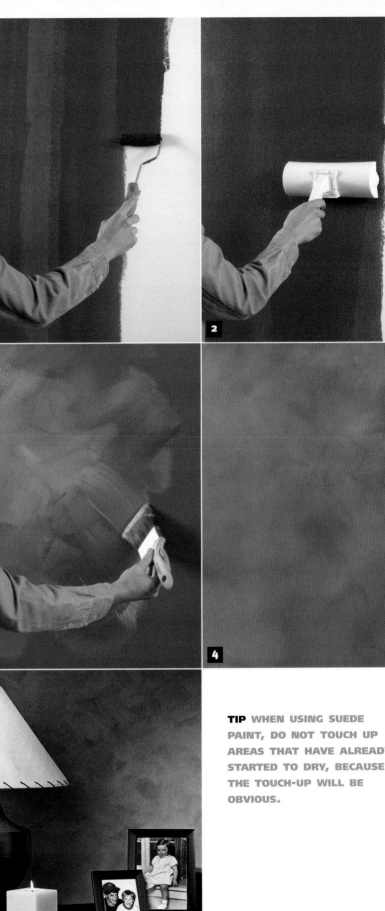

TIP WHEN USING SUEDE PAINT, DO NOT TOUCH UP AREAS THAT HAVE ALREADY STARTED TO DRY, BECAUSE THE TOUCH-UP WILL BE OBVIOUS.

silkfinish

A special metallic pearlescent silk paint is the secret to this elegant silk fabric look *below*. To achieve the effect, drag a wallpaper paste brush vertically in one continuous motion through a wet top coat of silk paint. The brush will reveal fine lines of the base color, exuding a soft, shimmering finish. It's best to section the walls off into vertical panels, allowing you to work quickly while the paint is wet. Complete opposite walls the same day and remaining walls the next day so you don't mar the wet glaze on adjacent walls. The glistening finish adds luxury and elegance to a living room, dining room, or bedroom. Dramatic lighting enhances the silk effect.

SKILL LEVEL Beginner

TOOLS YOU'LL NEED

PALE GREEN SEMIGLOSS FINISH LATEX PAINT FOR BASE COAT; METALLIC PEARL SILK PAINT

2-INCH LOW-TACK PAINTER'S TAPE (A)

DROP CLOTH

STIR STICKS

PAINT TRAY

STANDARD ROLLER FRAME WITH 9-INCH ROLLER COVER

2-INCH TAPERED TRIM BRUSH

LEVEL WITH PRINTED RULER (B)

GREEN COLORED PENCIL

PLASTIC CONTAINER WITH PRINTED MEASUREMENTS

GLAZE MEDIUM (C)

WALLPAPER PASTE BRUSH (D)

LINT-FREE COTTON CLOTHS

PALE GREEN LATEX PAINT AND METALLIC PEARL SILK PAINT

INSTRUCTIONS

Mask ceiling, baseboards, and trim with painter's tape. Paint the entire wall in the pale green base coat color. Paint two coats if necessary. Leave tape on; let dry overnight.

1

Divide the wall into vertical sections about 36 inches wide. Use a green colored pencil and level with ruler to measure and mark sections and extend the lines vertically.

2

Tape off alternating sections with painter's tape. Keep the tape just outside the colored pencil line and press down firmly on the tape to prevent the paint from bleeding underneath. In a plastic container, mix 1 part metallic silk paint and 1 part glaze.

3

Roll the glaze onto the first panel, smoothing the glaze out by rolling vertically until the glaze is coated evenly.

4 5 6

Drag the dry wallpaper paste brush through the glaze from top to bottom in one continuous motion, creating a vertical pattern in the wet glaze. Wipe excess glaze off the brush with a lint-free cloth and repeat until the panel is complete. Allow the panel to dry; then remove the tape.

Move to the next panel and repeat steps 3–6. After the panels dry, repeat steps 2–6. Remove remaining tape; allow to dry.

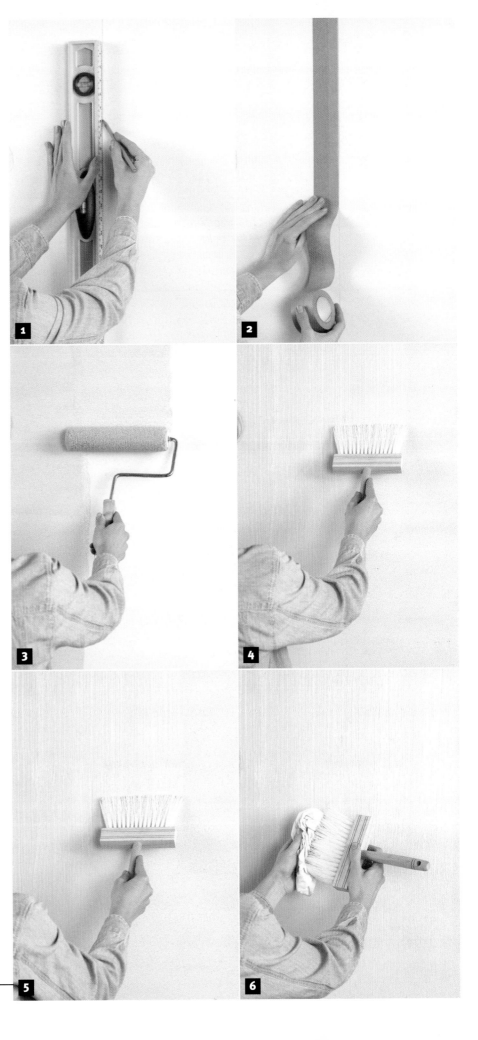

strié finish

The strié technique, also called dragging, gives your room the illusion of height with a pattern of thin vertical lines on the wall. To achieve this effect, roll glaze onto the wall in vertical taped-off sections. After the glaze is rolled on, immediately drag a long-bristle brush vertically through the glaze. The brush will remove some of the glaze, leaving thin lines on the wall that allow the base color to show through. This textured effect gives the impression of a finely woven fabric. Use this technique to add a stately, elegant wall finish to a living room, dining room, or bedroom. For a subtle effect, choose two different values of one color. For a more striking effect, select two high-contrasting colors.

SKILL LEVEL Beginner

TOOLS YOU'LL NEED

LIGHT BEIGE SEMIGLOSS FINISH LATEX PAINT FOR BASE COAT; MEDIUM BEIGE SEMIGLOSS FINISH LATEX PAINT FOR GLAZE COAT

LOW-TACK PAINTER'S TAPE (A)

DROP CLOTH

STIR STICKS

PAINT TRAY

STANDARD ROLLER FRAME WITH 9-INCH ROLLER COVER

2-INCH TAPERED TRIM BRUSH

LEVEL WITH PRINTED RULER (B)

LIGHT BROWN OR GRAY COLORED PENCIL

GLAZE MEDIUM (C)

PLASTIC CONTAINER WITH PRINTED MEASUREMENTS

STRIÉ BRUSH (D)

LINT-FREE COTTON CLOTHS

LIGHT BEIGE AND MEDIUM BEIGE LATEX PAINTS

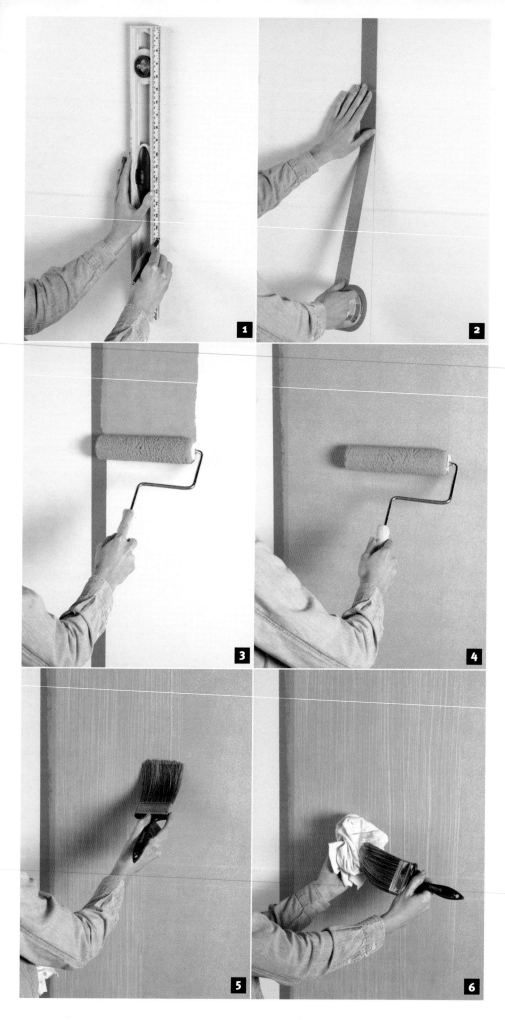

INSTRUCTIONS

Mask ceiling, baseboards, and trim with painter's tape.

Paint the entire wall in the light beige base coat color. Paint two coats if necessary. Leave tape on; let dry overnight.

Divide the wall into vertical panels for ease of glazing. The panels shown are approximately 30 inches wide. Using the level with printed ruler, measure and mark the panel widths across the wall.

1

Extend your measurements vertically, using the level and a colored pencil.

2

Tape off alternating sections with painter's tape. Burnish the edges by pressing down hard on the tape to prevent the paint from bleeding underneath.

Mix 4 parts glaze to 1 part medium beige paint in a plastic container.

3 **4**

Working quickly, trim and roll the glaze onto one vertical section. Roll through the glaze a second time to ensure an even coating.

5

Starting at the top of the just-glazed section, drag a strié brush through the glaze vertically. You do not have to drag the brush in one continuous line but try to stagger the stopping points.

Continue in this manner until the entire panel is finished.

6

Use a cloth to wipe excess glaze off the brush after each stroke.

7

Tape off each remaining panel. Use the same rolling and dragging process until all the panels are completed. Remove all tape and let dry.

TIPS WHEN DRAGGING THE BRUSH VERTICALLY, KEEP THE BRISTLES PARALLEL TO THE SURFACE.

WORK WITH A PARTNER AND HAVE ONE PERSON ROLL ON THE GLAZE AND THE OTHER PERSON QUICKLY DRAG THE BRUSH THROUGH THE GLAZE. WORK WITHOUT STOPPING UNTIL ONE WALL IS DONE.

THIS CAN BE A MESSY TECHNIQUE, SO USE PLENTY OF DROP CLOTHS TO PROTECT YOUR WORK AREA.

striéfinishvariations

1 Two similar shades of red provide a low-contrast, strié effect in this traditional-style bedroom. The finish is quite subtle and is best appreciated up close.

2 A strié paint finish is appropriate for any size room. In this small bath, the high-contrast red over white paint accentuates the textured appearance, giving the walls a streaky look.

3 Green strié walls and traditional furniture blend together for an elegant look in this dining room.

The finish complements the sunny yellow walls in the adjoining foyer and living room, allowing the paint colors to harmonize from room to room. White trim unifies the rooms as well.

4 The light green strié walls in this bedroom provide a delicately textured background for dark furniture and light-color accessories. Wall color can be inspired by an accessory item. In this case, the lamp inspired the celery green walls.

1

2 **3**

gingham finish

If you like the casual look of gingham fabric, try this pattern on your wall. Simply use a squeegee with ¾-inch notches to create the checked design. Drag the squeegee vertically and then horizontally through wet glaze. Subtle flaws are acceptable, so don't worry if your technique isn't perfect. To give the pattern a hand-painted feel, gently waver the lines as you pull the squeegee through the glaze. This design works best in rooms with few windows or doors. The bold pattern can be somewhat overwhelming, so try it under a chair rail or as a focal point on a solid wall. Or soften the pattern using a pastel palette.

SKILL LEVEL Beginner

TOOLS YOU'LL NEED

LAVENDER SATIN FINISH LATEX PAINT FOR BASE COAT; PALE LAVENDER SATIN FINISH LATEX PAINT FOR GLAZE COAT

2-INCH LOW-TACK PAINTER'S TAPE (A)

DROP CLOTH

STIR STICKS

PAINT TRAY

STANDARD ROLLER FRAME WITH 9-INCH ROLLER COVER

2-INCH TAPERED TRIM BRUSH

RULER

FINE-TIP MARKER

NOTCHED SQUEEGEE, 8 INCHES WIDE, AND CRAFTS KNIFE (B)

SELF-HEALING CUTTING MAT

GLAZE MEDIUM (C)

PLASTIC CONTAINER WITH PRINTED MEASUREMENTS

4-INCH FLAT PAINTBRUSH

LINT-FREE COTTON CLOTHS

LAVENDER AND PALE LAVENDER LATEX PAINTS

INSTRUCTIONS

Mask ceiling, baseboards, and trim with painter's tape. Paint the entire wall in the lavender base coat color. Paint two coats if necessary. Remove tape and let dry overnight.

Tape off a 4-foot section of wall. Use a ruler and fine-tip marker to divide the blade of the squeegee into ¾-inch sections. Cut out alternating sections with a crafts knife. Use a safe cutting surface, such as a self-healing cutting mat.

1

Mix 5 parts glaze to 1 part pale lavender paint in a plastic container. Roll on the pale lavender glaze.

2

Cut in along the wainscoting and baseboard and in the corners with a paintbrush.

3

While the glaze is still wet, start at the top of the section and pull the squeegee down the wall, making vertical stripes. Wipe excess glaze off the squeegee with a clean cloth. Repeat across the section, working quickly.

4

Start at the top of the wall and quickly drag the tool across the previously combed area to create horizontal stripes. Let the glaze dry and remove the tape.

5

Continue to tape and comb the walls until all the walls are finished. Allow to dry; remove all tape.

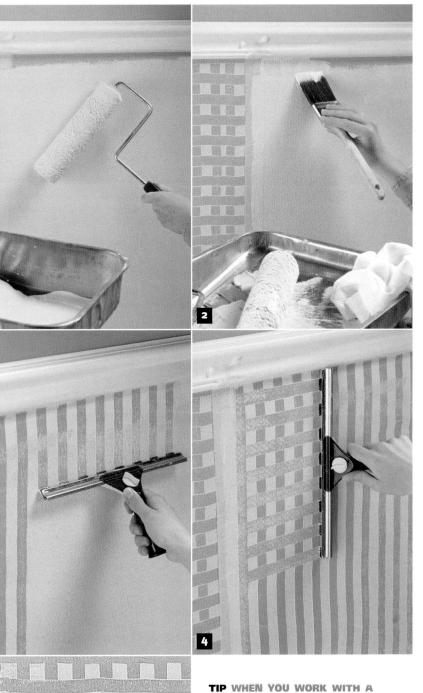

TIP WHEN YOU WORK WITH A SQUEEGEE, START IN A CORNER TO ENSURE A STRAIGHT LINE.

grasscloth

Painted grass cloth can be a stylish substitute for the wallcovering that was popular in the 1950s and is now making a comeback. Faux grass cloth allows you to vary the colors to suit your decor. To create the effect, drag a notched squeegee horizontally across the wet glazed surface, overlapping the squeegee pulls to create a continuous pattern. Depending on the width of the notches in the squeegee, the effect may resemble bamboo or rattan. A variation of the technique (see *page 83*) is created by dragging the squeegee through the glaze both horizontally and vertically. Follow the instructions for Burlap (see *page 60*), but vary the sizes of the squeegee notches from $\frac{1}{16}$ inch to $\frac{1}{4}$ inch to create finer, more randomly spaced lines.

SKILL LEVEL Intermediate

TOOLS YOU'LL NEED

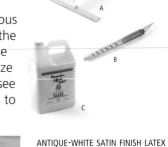

ANTIQUE-WHITE SATIN FINISH LATEX PAINT FOR BASE COAT; WARM OLIVE, GREENISH GRAY, AND MOSSY BROWN SATIN FINISH LATEX PAINTS FOR GLAZE COAT

2-INCH LOW-TACK PAINTER'S TAPE

DROP CLOTH

STIR STICKS

PAINT TRAY

STANDARD ROLLER FRAME WITH 9-INCH ROLLER COVER

2-INCH TAPERED TRIM BRUSH

4-INCH CHIP BRUSH

METAL YARDSTICK

PENCIL

RULER

FINE-TIP MARKER

SQUEEGEE (A)

CRAFTS KNIFE (B)

SELF-HEALING CUTTING MAT

GLAZE MEDIUM (C)

3 PLASTIC CONTAINERS WITH PRINTED MEASUREMENTS

LINT-FREE COTTON CLOTHS

ANTIQUE-WHITE, WARM OLIVE, GREENISH GRAY, AND MOSSY BROWN LATEX PAINTS

HEATH'S FERN PORTFOLIO.

INSTRUCTIONS

Mask ceiling, baseboards, and trim with painter's tape. Paint the entire wall in the antique-white base coat color. Paint two coats if necessary. Leave tape on; allow to dry overnight.

Use a ruler and fine-tip marker to divide the blade of the squeegee into ½-inch sections. Cut out a small notch, approximately ⅛-inch-wide, at every mark with a crafts knife. Use a safe cutting surface, such as a self-healing cutting mat.

1

Use a metal yardstick and pencil to mark the wall off in 3-foot-wide sections. Tape off alternating vertical sections with 2-inch painter's tape.

Use a plastic container to mix 4 parts glaze to 1 part warm olive paint. Use the same process to make two additional glazes using greenish gray paint and mossy brown paint.

2

Dip the chip brush into varying combinations of glazes. Start at the top of the wall and brush glaze on the first taped-off section using a horizontal motion.

3

While the glaze is still wet, place the squeegee on top of the taped edge and drag horizontally until you reach the opposite edge, pulling the squeegee onto the tape. Wipe excess glaze onto a cloth after each pass. Overlap the squeegee pulls to create a continuous pattern.

4

Using the chip brush, lightly dry-brush the lines in a horizontal motion to blend and soften.

5

Move down the wall and brush on the glaze with the chip brush. Overlap your brush strokes into

the previously glazed section to create a continuous pattern.

6

Drag the squeegee horizontally through the glaze in the same manner as in Step 4. If glaze becomes too dry to produce continuous lines, add a small amount of water to your mixtures and reapply the glaze to that section with a chip brush. This will dampen the surface and allow a clean sweep with the squeegee.

7

Lightly soften the lines with the chip brush, using a horizontal motion before the glaze dries. Continue until you've finished the section. Allow to dry.

8

Tape off remaining sections. Repeat the process until the wall is completed. Remove remaining tape; allow to dry.

GRASS-CLOTH VARIATION USING SMALLER PANELS AND NARROWER LINES IN BROWN.

GRASS-CLOTH VARIATION USING A RED OIL GLAZE OVER A BEIGE BASE COAT.

wickertexture

If you like the exotic look of bamboo furniture, try this wicker-inspired technique. A brown gel stain applied over a golden peach base coat blends to create a warm bamboo color. A notched squeegee pulled vertically and then horizontally through the stain brings out the wicker texture. Use a steady hand when using the squeegee. A corner or doorway will provide a hard edge to guide the first pull. It's also helpful to mark vertical lines across the wall every three inches to use as a guideline to ensure straight pulls. For consistency across the wall, overlap the pulls by one line to create a continuous pattern of lines. Faux wicker creates a casual garden-room look and is effective below a chair rail as in the living area *below*.

SKILL LEVEL Intermediate

TOOLS YOU'LL NEED

GOLDEN PEACH SATIN FINISH LATEX PAINT FOR BASE COAT

2-INCH LOW-TACK PAINTER'S TAPE

DROP CLOTH

STIR STICKS

PAINT TRAY

STANDARD ROLLER FRAME WITH 9-INCH ROLLER COVER

2-INCH TAPERED TRIM BRUSH

RULER

FINE-TIP MARKER

SQUEEGEE (A)

CRAFTS KNIFE (B)

SELF-HEALING CUTTING MAT

METAL YARDSTICK (C)

GRAPHITE PENCIL

BROWN GEL STAIN (D)

RUBBER GLOVES

2-INCH CHIP BRUSH

LINT-FREE COTTON CLOTHS

GOLDEN PEACH
LATEX PAINT

INSTRUCTIONS

Mask the chair rail and baseboard. Paint below the chair rail in the golden peach color. Paint two coats if necessary. Leave the tape on; let dry overnight.

Use a ruler and fine-tip marker to divide the blade of the squeegee into alternating ⅛- and ¼-inch sections. Cut out the ¼-inch sections with a crafts knife. Leave the ⅛-inch sections intact. Use a safe cutting surface, such as a self-healing cutting mat.

1

Mark off guidelines in 18-inch-wide sections with a metal yardstick and pencil. Wearing rubber gloves and starting in the first section, apply gel stain with a 2-inch chip brush working in vertical strokes.

2

Starting at the bottom edge of the chair rail, drag the squeegee vertically from top to bottom in one continuous motion. Use both hands for more stability. Wipe excess gel stain from the squeegee with a cloth.

3

Starting at the bottom edge of the chair rail, drag the squeegee horizontally across alternating vertical lines. Leave the last line unmarked to use as a guide for your next vertical pull. Use the bottom horizontal-dashed lines to guide you as you move down the wall. Wipe excess gel stain from the squeegee with a cloth.

4

Move to the next section and brush on stain. Brush over the raw edge of the previously stained section but

not into the previously dragged area. Drag the squeegee vertically from top to bottom through the stain.

5

Drag the squeegee horizontally across alternating vertical lines. Overlap the top edge of the squeegee with the bottom line of the previous pull. Wipe excess gel stain from the squeegee as needed.

Repeat on remaining sections until the wall is completed. Remove tape; allow to dry.

wood-grainmoiré

The wood-grain moiré pattern that complements the wall in the living area *below* is easy to reproduce using a special wood-graining tool available at most crafts stores and home centers. Simply position the tool at the top of the wall and use a dragging and rocking motion as you pull it through a top coat of wet glaze. As it moves down the wall, a moiré pattern will emerge, exposing the base color underneath. A steady hand is required for this technique. Practice on a sample board until you are comfortable with the dragging motion. Medium blue and pale blue were used under this chair rail, but try tan and walnut for a rustic effect.

SKILL LEVEL Beginner

TOOLS YOU'LL NEED

PALE BLUE SATIN FINISH LATEX PAINT FOR BASE COAT; MEDIUM BLUE SATIN FINISH LATEX PAINT FOR GLAZE COAT

2-INCH LOW-TACK PAINTER'S TAPE

DROP CLOTH

STIR STICKS

PAINT TRAY

STANDARD ROLLER FRAME WITH 9-INCH ROLLER COVER (A)

2-INCH TAPERED TRIM BRUSH

GLAZE MEDIUM (B)

PLASTIC CONTAINER WITH PRINTED MEASUREMENTS

WOOD-GRAINING TOOL (C)

LINT-FREE COTTON CLOTHS (D)

PALE BLUE AND MEDIUM BLUE LATEX PAINTS

INSTRUCTIONS

Mask chair rail and baseboards with painter's tape. Paint the entire wall in the pale blue base color. Paint two coats if necessary. Leave tape on; let dry overnight.

1

Mix 4 parts glaze with 1 part medium blue paint in a plastic container. Working quickly, roll a narrow width of glaze mixture onto the wall.

2

Starting at the top of the wall, pull the wood-graining tool down the wall. Rock the tool up and down along the way. As you do this, slightly overlap the previous "plank."

3

Use a dry cloth to clean excess glaze off the graining tool.

4

Continue this process of rolling glaze onto the wall, then removing with the wood-graining tool, until the wall is completed. Remove all tape; allow to dry.

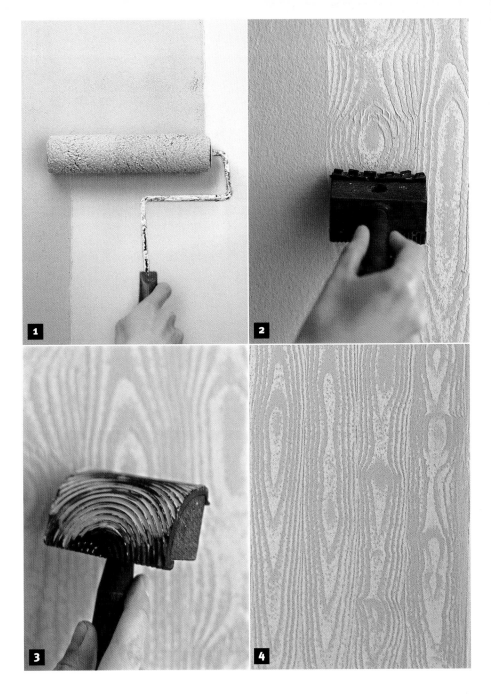

marblefinish

Marbling is one of the more elegant and popular faux finishes. You can now create a realistic marbling effect due to an innovative approach to the technique. Instead of sponging layers of paint on the wall, apply paint to a piece of heavy plastic using a chip brush, blending the colors slightly. Press the plastic to the wall, to create random, irregular shapes. To make the veins, pull an artist's brush through the paint. Veins can be thicker in some areas and thinner in others. Use contrasting colors with many layers for more drama. Soft colors and fewer layers produce a more subtle result. It's best to practice on a sample board before you try it on the wall.

SKILL LEVEL Advanced

TOOLS YOU'LL NEED

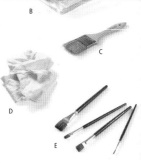

WHITE SEMIGLOSS FINISH LATEX PAINT FOR BASE COAT; WHITE, YELLOW OCHER, AND RAW UMBER ARTIST'S OIL PAINTS

2-INCH LOW-TACK PAINTER'S TAPE

DROP CLOTH

STIR STICKS

PAINT TRAY

STANDARD ROLLER WITH 9-INCH ROLLER COVER

2-INCH TAPERED TRIM BRUSH

PLASTIC CONTAINER WITH PRINTED MEASUREMENTS

LIQUIN ARTIST'S MEDIUM (A)

PLASTIC, 1 MILLIMETER THICK (B)

THREE 2-INCH CHIP BRUSHES (C)

LINT-FREE COTTON CLOTHS (D)

ARTIST'S BRUSHES, INCLUDING A WIDE, FLAT BRUSH; SMALL LINER BRUSH; AND 1/2-INCH FLAT DETAIL BRUSH (E)

PAINT THINNER (MINERAL SPIRITS)

WHITE LATEX PAINT; WHITE, YELLOW OCHER, AND RAW UMBER ARTIST'S PAINT

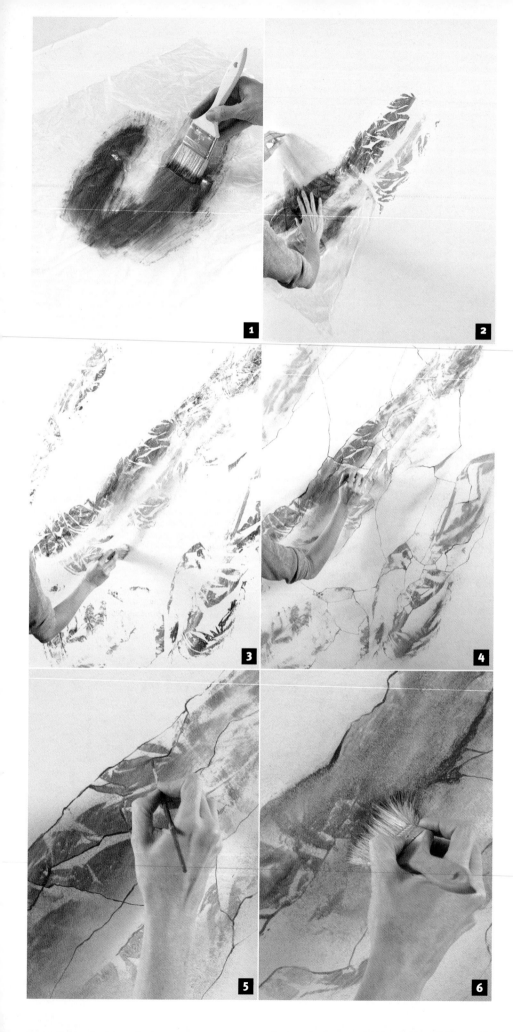

INSTRUCTIONS

Mask off the area you wish to marble with painter's tape. Paint the entire area in the white base coat color. Apply two coats if needed. Leave tape on; allow to dry.

1

Create thinned mixtures of each of the three oil colors by adding 1 part paint to 1 part Liquin. This will make the paint flow and give it transparency as well as shorten the drying time. You will only need small amounts of each color so mix as you go. Cut a 1×2-foot piece of plastic. Using a chip brush, apply white, raw umber, and yellow ocher paint to the plastic, keeping your brushstrokes flowing in one direction and allowing the colors to blend slightly.

2

Determine the direction and angle you want the marble to flow and lightly place the plastic on the surface, paint side down. Let the plastic cling to create random, irregular shapes and gently press it to the wall with your hand. Peel it off and shift it to a new area and repeat. You should be able to repeat this process two to four more times before adding more paint. Press more firmly with each repeat.

3

With a clean, dry chip brush, blend and soften selected areas using a stippling motion, dabbing up and down. Occasionally wipe your brush on a clean cotton cloth to remove excess paint.

4

Use a thin liner brush to create thin veins, connecting the shapes you've created with the plastic. Vary your veins by using various mixtures of the three oil colors and alternating the pressure of your brush to create light, thin veins or dark, heavy ones. Add more Liquin to produce fainter veins.

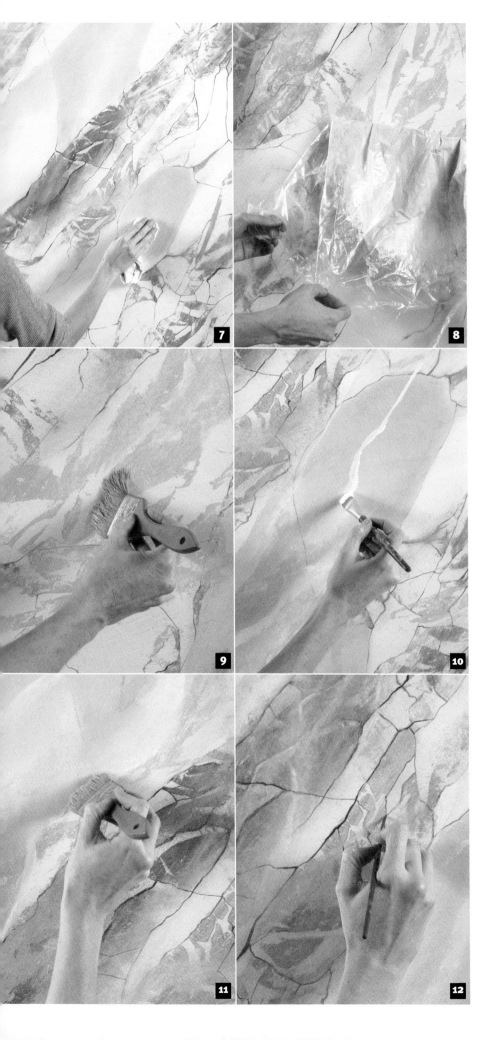

5
Detail of Step 4.

6
With a clean, dry chip brush, blend and soften the veins using a stippling motion. Occasionally wipe the brush on a clean cotton cloth.

7
Use a clean cotton cloth to rub on a light mixture of white, yellow ocher, and raw umber in the larger empty areas.

8
Add layers by repeating Step 2, but use lighter-color mixtures, such as 1 part white with 1 part ocher or simply pure white oil paint.

9
Blend fresh applications using a dry, clean chip brush.

10
Dip a ½-inch flat detail brush into the white oil paint to create bolder, dramatic veins.

11
Soften the veins with a chip brush.

12
Retrace some of the darker, finer veins that may be too soft and create new sharp veins with a thin liner brush.

Continue until you reach the desired results. Remove all tape; allow to dry. When completed, clean the brushes in paint thinner.

TIP REPEAT ANY PROCESS TO REACH THE DESIRED RESULT. IF THE FINISHED PROJECT IS TOO DRAMATIC AND DARK, FOR EXAMPLE, ALLOW THE PAINT TO DRY AND WASH THE ENTIRE SURFACE WITH A THIN MIXTURE OF WHITE. THIS WILL SOFTEN AND COOL DOWN THE COLORS. BLEND THE COLORS BEFORE THEY DRY TO AVOID HARD EDGES.

marblefinishvariations

1 Faux-marble veining in white, black, and red highlight the recessed areas of the fireplace surround in this contemporary living room. The surrounding walls are painted with the same red in the marble effect.

2 Use yellow ocher and a little burnt umber for depth to achieve this honey-gold marble finish. Sketch the veins randomly and blend them well into the surrounding color for a soft, subtle effect.

3 The faux-marble panels below the chair rail bring a classic look to this living room. The base coat is made up of linen white, pale gold, and rosy peach oil paints. Gray-green veins are added with a cloth and soft-bristle brush.

4 The faux-marble walls in this bathroom started with a creamy base coat. Veins of rusty-peach glaze were added for the marble effect. To complement the walls, the woodwork and doors were painted a faux-maple wood grain.

limestonefinish

Creating the textured look of a limestone block wall is an updated application of an old technique, simple sponging. The keys to this more sophisticated approach are using a limited range of related colors and blending them on the sponge rather than on the wall. After dipping the sponge into the glaze, dab it onto a piece of cardboard to evenly distribute the paint across the surface of the sponge. This helps control the amount of paint applied to the wall. Applying the paint in blocks enhances the effect of a stone wall. These blocks are painted in a variety of sizes and staggered in their placement to add interest. Try this finish on other surfaces too—columns, fireplace surrounds, lamp bases, and large planters are all good candidates.

SKILL LEVEL Beginner

TOOLS YOU'LL NEED

ANTIQUE-WHITE FLAT FINISH LATEX PAINT FOR BASE COAT; WARM TAN AND PALE GOLD FLAT FINISH LATEX PAINTS FOR TEXTURE COAT

2-INCH LOW-TACK PAINTER'S TAPE

DROP CLOTH

STIR STICKS

PAINT TRAY

STANDARD ROLLER FRAME WITH 9-INCH ROLLER COVER

2-INCH TAPERED TRIM BRUSH

TAN COLORED PENCIL (A)

METAL YARDSTICK (B)

SEA SPONGE (C)

PLASTIC CONTAINER OF WATER

SCRAP FOAM CORE OR CARDBOARD

ANTIQUE WHITE, WARM TAN, AND PALE GOLD LATEX PAINTS

INSTRUCTIONS

Mask ceiling, baseboards, and trim with painter's tape. Paint the entire wall in the antique-white base coat color. Paint two coats if necessary. Leave tape on; let dry overnight.

Plan your block design by first determining the height of the blocks. The blocks shown are approximately 12 inches in height. Use a tan colored pencil to mark the horizontal lines. Mark off the vertical lines about every 20 inches, staggering them from row to row to create a stacked block effect. Make heavy marks so you can use them as a guide as you paint.

1

Dip the sea sponge into a plastic container of water and squeeze out the excess water. Sponge on varying mixtures of warm tan and antique white, leaving most of the wall surface untouched. Dip the sponge into one color, then the other, alternating colors. Tap onto scrap foam core or cardboard to blend and distribute paint evenly on the sponge before applying to the wall.

2

Sponge on varying mixtures of warm tan and pale gold, covering selected areas more heavily than others but keeping the overall effect airy. Rinse out the sponge.

3

Sponge antique white evenly but sparingly over the entire surface. Be careful not to cover the guidelines completely. Allow to dry. Lightly retrace any lines that may be covered with paint.

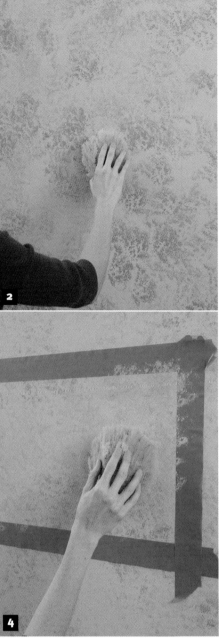

4

Tape off random blocks with painter's tape. Continue to sponge on various combinations of color. Concentrate on emphasizing edges with either dark or light applications. Remove tape; allow to dry. Tape new blocks and repeat.

5

When you have finished painting, you may need to go back and darken or lighten selected edges of blocks for more or less drama. Remove all tape; allow to dry.

stoneblocks

A textured stone-block effect gives a stunning look to this entryway *below* using a simple technique called *frottage*, from the French word "frotter," which means "to rub." The technique involves pressing a newspaper onto a glazed wall with your hands. For the stone-block look, a space between newspaper applications creates a mortar effect. If you prefer an overall textured appearance, use a full-size newspaper and place it on the wall so that it slightly overlaps the previous application.

SKILL LEVEL Beginner

TOOLS YOU'LL NEED

A

B

LIGHT IVORY SATIN FINISH LATEX PAINT FOR BASE COAT; BEIGE SATIN FINISH LATEX PAINT FOR GLAZE COAT

2-INCH LOW-TACK PAINTER'S TAPE

DROP CLOTH

STIR STICKS

PAINT TRAY

STANDARD ROLLER FRAME WITH 9-INCH ROLLER COVER

2-INCH TAPERED TRIM BRUSH

NEWSPAPERS (A)

SCISSORS

GLAZE MEDIUM (B)

PLASTIC CONTAINER WITH PRINTED MEASUREMENTS

LIGHT IVORY AND BEIGE LATEX PAINTS

INSTRUCTIONS

Mask ceiling, baseboards, and trim with painter's tape. Paint the entire wall in the light ivory base coat color. Paint two coats if necessary. Leave tape on; let dry overnight.

Cut the newspaper pieces to the desired size or use them full size.

1

Mix 5 parts glaze to 1 part beige paint in a plastic container. Apply the glaze with a roller to an area approximately 4×4 feet.

2

While the glaze mixture is still wet, use both hands to press the newspaper onto the wall, overlapping and wrinkling it slightly with your hands.

3

Carefully remove the newspaper from the wall and discard. Leave a 1-inch space between the newspaper applications to create a faux mortar between the stones.

4

Continue across the entire wall, using a new piece of paper each time you remove glaze from the wall. Always be sure that there is wet glaze well beyond the edge of the newspaper so that it doesn't create starting and stopping points. Let each wall dry completely before starting the next to prevent smudging a corner. When finished, remove all tape and allow to dry.

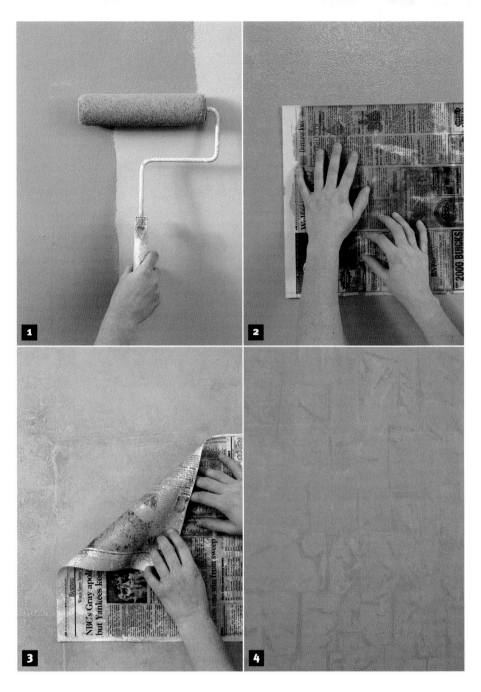

TIPS IF YOU ARE WORKING ON LARGE AREAS, IT MAY BE EASIER FOR TWO PEOPLE TO WORK TOGETHER, ONE APPLYING THE GLAZING MEDIUM AND THE OTHER CREATING THE DESIGN.

FOR A MORE TEXTURED APPEARANCE, APPLY A THICKER LAYER OF GLAZE.

WHEN YOU ARE APPLYING THE NEWSPAPER, USE FIRM PRESSURE WITH THE PALM OF YOUR HAND. BE CAREFUL NOT TO DRAG YOUR FINGERS, WHICH WILL CREATE UNDESIRABLE LINES. FINGERTIP PRINTS, HOWEVER, WILL ENHANCE THE DESIGN.

mottledsponging

Sponging is one of the simpler faux-finishing techniques to master.
You simply use a dampened sea sponge to apply glaze color over
a lighter base coat color, creating a mottled, dimensional look.
In this living area *opposite*, three shades of tan are sponged over
an off-white wall. It's best to choose similar rather than contrasting
colors when you sponge. To ensure a professional look, use small
pieces of sea sponge to fill in the corners and along the ceiling and
trimwork. Any blank spots will give the walls an unfinished look.

SKILL LEVEL Beginner

TOOLS YOU'LL NEED

A

B

C

OFF-WHITE SATIN FINISH LATEX
PAINT FOR BASE COAT; LIGHT
PEACHY TAN, MEDIUM PEACHY
TAN, AND DARK PEACHY TAN
SATIN FINISH LATEX PAINTS
FOR GLAZE COAT

2-INCH LOW-TACK PAINTER'S TAPE

DROP CLOTH

STIR STICKS

THREE PAINT TRAYS (A)

STANDARD ROLLER FRAME WITH
9-INCH ROLLER COVER

2-INCH TAPERED TRIM BRUSH

LARGE SEA SPONGE (B)

BUCKET OF WATER

LINT-FREE COTTON CLOTHS
OR PAPER TOWELS (C)

SMALL PIECES OF SEA SPONGE

OFF-WHITE, LIGHT PEACHY
TAN, MEDIUM PEACHY TAN,
AND DARK PEACHY TAN
LATEX PAINTS

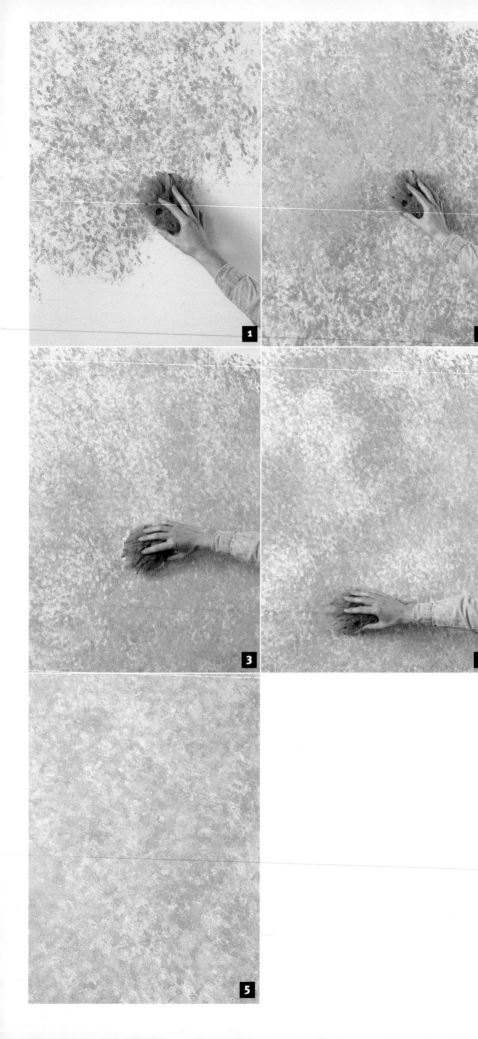

INSTRUCTIONS

Mask ceilings, baseboards, and trim with painter's tape. Paint the entire wall in the off-white base coat color. Paint two coats if necessary. Leave tape on; let dry overnight.

1

Pour a small amount of dark peachy tan (the darkest sponging color) into a clean paint tray. Wet the sea sponge with water and wring it out thoroughly. Dip the sponge into the dark peachy tan paint. Blot excess paint onto a cotton cloth or paper towel. Tap the sponge onto the wall, turning it each time you tap the wall to create an irregular, mottled effect. Overlap each impression for complete paint coverage. Apply paint to the corners using the small sponges. Continue dipping, blotting, and sponging until the wall is covered.

2

Apply the medium peachy tan color using the same technique. Sponge the corners last.

3

Sponge the light peachy tan color in the same manner.

4

Reapply the light peachy tan color where necessary to add dimension.

5

Repeat any of the other colors to achieve the desired effect. Continue this process until the entire wall is completed. Remove all tape; allow to dry.

TIPS STEP BACK AND REVIEW YOUR WORK OFTEN TO ENSURE A CONSISTENT LOOK. SPONGE THE PAINT ON LIGHTLY.

SPONGING IS A GREAT TECHNIQUE TO USE ON IMPERFECT WALLS BECAUSE IT WILL HIDE FLAWS.

mottledspongingvariations

1 The walls in this bedroom are sponged above the chair rail for a slightly mottled, antique effect. The subdued colors create a light, airy background for furniture and accessories.

2 Sponging stripes instead of simply painting them softens the hard lines and produces a more subtle effect. The muted stripes were created by sponging the entire wall with a cream color. After the stripes were taped off, green paint was gently sponged on for a slightly washed effect.

A thistle stencil applied to the green stripes in a slightly darker tone adds a custom-designed touch.

3 Using different kinds of sponges creates different effects. A sea sponge produced the mottled texture below the chair rail, while a honeycomb pad created a streaked horizontal look on the wall above the chair rail.

chamois aging

This basic ragging technique creates an aged effect that resembles the soft texture of chamois. The technique uses cotton cloths to blend different glaze colors over a base color, producing a soft mottled look on the wall. A chip brush is also used to stipple, or pounce, straight up and down over the surface to further blend the glazes. Ragging is suitable for all types of decor, but it is most often associated with country- or cottage-style decorating. When selecting the colors for your project, remember that similar colors will produce a quiet, subdued look, while contrasting colors will produce a more dramatic effect.

SKILL LEVEL Beginner

TOOLS YOU'LL NEED

A

B

C

ANTIQUE WHITE SATIN FINISH LATEX PAINT FOR BASE COAT; WARM TAN SATIN FINISH LATEX PAINT FOR GLAZE COAT

2-INCH LOW-TACK PAINTER'S TAPE

DROP CLOTH

STIR STICKS

PAINT TRAY

STANDARD ROLLER FRAME WITH 9-INCH ROLLER COVER

2-INCH TAPERED TRIM BRUSH

GLAZE MEDIUM (A)

PLASTIC CONTAINER WITH PRINTED MEASUREMENTS

LINT-FREE COTTON CLOTHS (B)

4-INCH CHIP BRUSH (C)

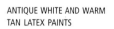

ANTIQUE WHITE AND WARM TAN LATEX PAINTS

INSTRUCTIONS

Mask ceiling, baseboards, and trim with painter's tape. Paint the entire wall in the antique-white base coat color. Paint two coats if necessary. Leave tape on; let dry overnight.

1

Mix 1 part warm tan to 4 parts glaze medium in a plastic container. Roll glaze onto an area approximately 3×3 feet, keeping the area organic with uneven edges and irregular shapes.

2

Use a clean cotton cloth to soften and blend the glaze. Feather or fade the edges first, then use the cloth in the center to avoid dark areas that overlap.

3

With a 4-inch chip brush, stipple and continue to soften the glaze. Continue this process until the wall is completed.

4

Mix 1 part antique white to 4 parts glaze medium. Lightly brush on selected areas with a 4-inch chip brush.

5

Soften and blend edges with a clean cloth as you go. Slightly dampen the cloth as necessary.

6

Continue this process until the wall is completed. Remove all tape; allow to dry.

TIP RESHAPING YOUR CLOTH CAN PRODUCE A VARIETY OF TEXTURES. PRACTICE SHAPING YOUR CLOTH UNTIL YOU ACHIEVE THE DESIRED EFFECT.

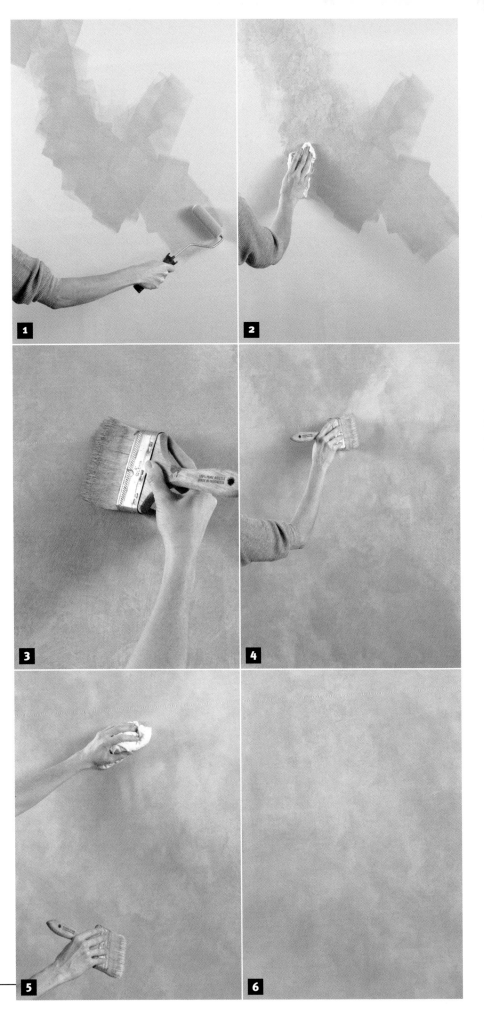

amberaging

The amber aging effect covers the wall *below* with a warm golden tone that accentuates both the light-color arched windows and the dark stairway handrail and posts. For this technique, a gold glaze is blended and softened using a cotton cloth. The edges are feathered for a consistent finish. When you are rolling on the glaze, keep the working areas organic with irregular shapes and uneven edges. Avoid rolling over sections that have already been ragged and feathered. To add richness to the surface, apply mahogany stain with a chip brush and blend with a clean cloth. This effect is perfect for an area calling for drama, such as a hallway or alcove.

SKILL LEVEL Beginner

TOOLS YOU'LL NEED

A

B

C

CREAMY YELLOW SATIN FINISH LATEX PAINT FOR BASE COAT; GOLD SATIN FINISH LATEX PAINT FOR GLAZE COAT

2-INCH LOW-TACK PAINTER'S TAPE

DROP CLOTH

STIR STICKS

PAINT TRAY

STANDARD ROLLER WITH 9-INCH ROLLER COVER

2-INCH TAPERED TRIM BRUSH

GLAZE MEDIUM (A)

PLASTIC CONTAINER WITH PRINTED MEASUREMENTS

MINI ROLLER FRAME WITH 4-INCH ROLLER COVER

LINT-FREE COTTON CLOTHS

4-INCH CHIP BRUSH (B)

MAHOGANY GEL STAIN (C)

CREAMY YELLOW AND GOLD LATEX PAINTS

INSTRUCTIONS

Mask ceiling, baseboards, and trim with painter's tape. Paint the entire wall in the creamy yellow base coat color. Paint two coats if necessary. Leave tape on; let dry overnight.

1

Mix 1 part gold to 4 parts glaze medium in a plastic container. Using a mini roller, apply glaze on an area approximately 3×3 feet, keeping areas organic.

2

Use a clean cotton cloth to soften and blend the glaze. Feather or fade the edges first, then rag in the center to eliminate overlapping areas. Allow to dry. Repeat this process until the wall is completed.

3

With a 4-inch chip brush, apply mahogany stain to small areas at a time.

4

Blend and soften the stain with a clean cotton cloth. Continue to build up stain so that it is heavier in some areas and lighter in others, allowing stain to dry between applications.

5

Continue this process until you achieve the desired effect. Remove all tape; allow to dry.

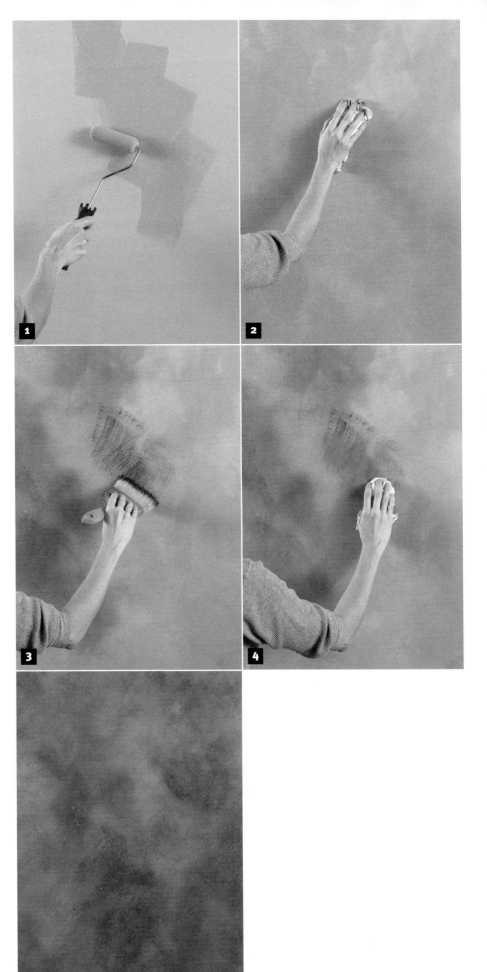

old-world aging

The aged walls in the elegant hallway *below* were created by using a trowel to apply several coats of paint. The walls are first layered in three glaze colors then blended with a slightly dampened cloth. The layers are heavier in some areas than others to add dimension. Antique-white paint is then trowelled directly onto the surface, giving the walls a coarse, plaster-like finish. This effect mimics old plaster walls found in a European manor.

SKILL LEVEL Advanced

TOOLS YOU'LL NEED

ANTIQUE WHITE, WARM TAN, AND COOL TAN SATIN FINISH LATEX PAINTS

2-INCH LOW-TACK PAINTER'S TAPE

DROP CLOTH

STIR STICKS

PAINT TRAY

STANDARD ROLLER FRAME WITH 9-INCH ROLLER COVER

2-INCH TAPERED TRIM BRUSH

GLAZE MEDIUM (A)

2 PLASTIC CONTAINERS WITH PRINTED MEASUREMENTS

ROLLER FRAME WITH 6-INCH SPONGE ROLLER COVER (B)

LINT-FREE COTTON CLOTHS (C)

METAL TROWEL (D)

2-INCH CHIP BRUSH

ANTIQUE WHITE, WARM TAN, AND COOL TAN LATEX PAINTS

INSTRUCTIONS

Mask ceiling, baseboards, and trim with painter's tape. Paint the entire wall in the antique-white base coat color. Paint two coats if necessary. Leave tape on; let dry overnight.

1

Mix two separate glazes of cool tan and warm tan, using 1 part paint to 4 parts glaze medium. Randomly roll on the glazes with a sponge roller, working in one small area at a time.

2

Using a slightly damp cotton cloth, soften the glazes. Slightly feather the edges so the working areas blend together. Leave the application heavier in some areas to add dimension.

3

Trowel on unthinned antique white paint, applying it more thickly at the top of the wall and more sparingly toward the bottom. Skip the metal trowel lightly across the surface for a plaster look. Use a chip brush and the short end of the trowel to vary the surface.

4

Dip a damp cotton cloth into the antique-white paint and wash selected areas to soften and fade. Allow to dry.

5

Add glaze to the cool tan mixture so it is thinned to approximately 1 part paint to 6 parts glaze. Rub on with a clean damp cotton cloth, varying the application so the color is thinner in some areas and thicker in others.

6

Continue until the wall is completed. Remove all tape; allow to dry.

crackleaging

Crackled walls give rooms a rustic, country look. To create the effect, select contrasting paint colors for the base and top coats. The crackling is caused by applying a crackle medium between the two layers of paint. The medium causes the top coat of paint to dry faster than the bottom coat and to shrink, exposing the base color underneath. If the crackle medium is brushed on, the cracks will follow the direction of the brush marks. If the medium is rolled on, it will crackle in a uniform pattern. Crackling is also an effective way to add character to furniture, trim, molding, and accessories, such as picture frames.

SKILL LEVEL Beginner

TOOLS YOU'LL NEED

WHITE SATIN FINISH LATEX PAINT FOR BASE COAT; RED SATIN FINISH LATEX PAINT FOR TOP COAT

2-INCH LOW-TACK PAINTER'S TAPE

DROP CLOTH

STIR STICKS

PAINT TRAY

STANDARD ROLLER FRAME WITH 9-INCH ROLLER COVER (A)

2-INCH TAPERED TRIM BRUSH (B)

CRACKLE MEDIUM (C)

WHITE AND RED LATEX PAINTS

INSTRUCTIONS

Mask ceiling, baseboards, and trim with painter's tape. Paint the entire wall in the white base coat color. Paint two coats if necessary. Leave tape on; let dry overnight.

1

Roll crackle medium evenly onto the wall with the roller. Fill in the edges and corners with the trim brush. Try to keep the application uniform. Allow to dry.

2

Working on one wall at a time, roll on the top coat of red paint and paint the corners and edges with the trim brush. Do not overlap or rebrush the top coat of paint after the paint has started to crack. Touch-ups will be obvious and will not crack again. The secret is to move quickly. It's acceptable to use a combination of rolling and brushing to apply the top coat.

3

Repeat the process for each wall to crackle the remaining walls. Remove all tape; allow to dry.

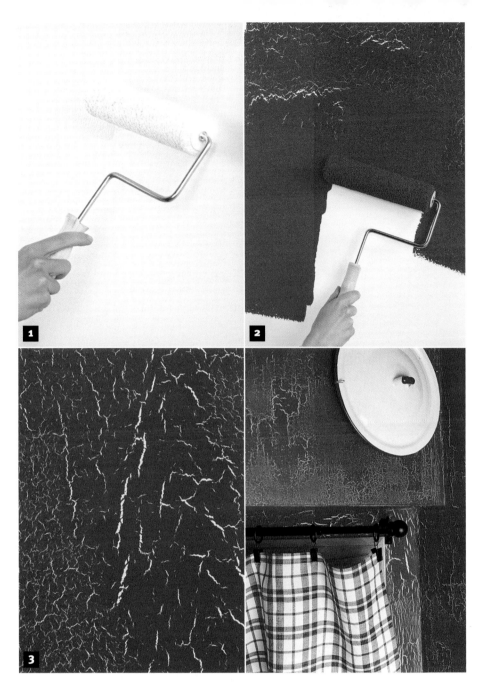

TIPS THE THICKNESS OF THE TOP COAT OF PAINT WILL DEFINE THE SIZE OF THE CRACKS. A THIN LAYER WILL RESULT IN SMALLER, FINER CRACKS. A HEAVIER APPLICATION WILL RESULT IN LARGER CRACKS.

PRACTICE THIS TECHNIQUE ON A PIECE OF SCRAP BOARD OR FOAM CORE BEFORE APPLYING PAINT TO THE WALL. THIS WILL ALSO GIVE YOU A CHANCE TO PREVIEW YOUR SELECTION OF COLORS.

IT'S A GOOD IDEA TO RECRUIT A FRIEND IF YOU ARE CRACKLING A LARGE AREA.

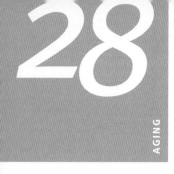

distressedaging

The natural look of distressing, often used to give furniture a gently worn appearance, can be created on any surface. To achieve this effect, some aging techniques use sandpaper to expose contrasting coats of paint, but the weathered look shown here is achieved by using a simple paint technique. Several layers of glaze are applied to the door, and a wood graining tool is dragged and rocked through the glaze to create a dimensional, raised-grain appearance. Remember that the aged look should be simulated in places where natural wear will normally occur, such as in corners, on raised portions, and around door handles. This look is often used in country decorating schemes, but it can also work successfully with other decorating styles.

SKILL LEVEL Intermediate

TOOLS YOU'LL NEED

WHITE SATIN FINISH LATEX PAINT FOR BASE COAT; LIGHT BROWN AND BLUE-GRAY SATIN FINISH LATEX PAINTS FOR GLAZE COAT

2-INCH LOW-TACK PAINTER'S TAPE

DROP CLOTH

STIR STICKS

PAINT TRAY

2-INCH TAPERED TRIM BRUSH

GLAZE MEDIUM (A)

PLASTIC CONTAINER WITH PRINTED MEASUREMENTS

TWO 2-INCH CHIP BRUSHES (B)

WOOD-GRAINING TOOL (C)

LINT-FREE COTTON CLOTHS (D)

2-INCH PLASTIC TROWEL (E)

SCRAP BOARD OR FOAM CORE

WHITE, LIGHT BROWN, AND BLUE-GRAY LATEX PAINTS

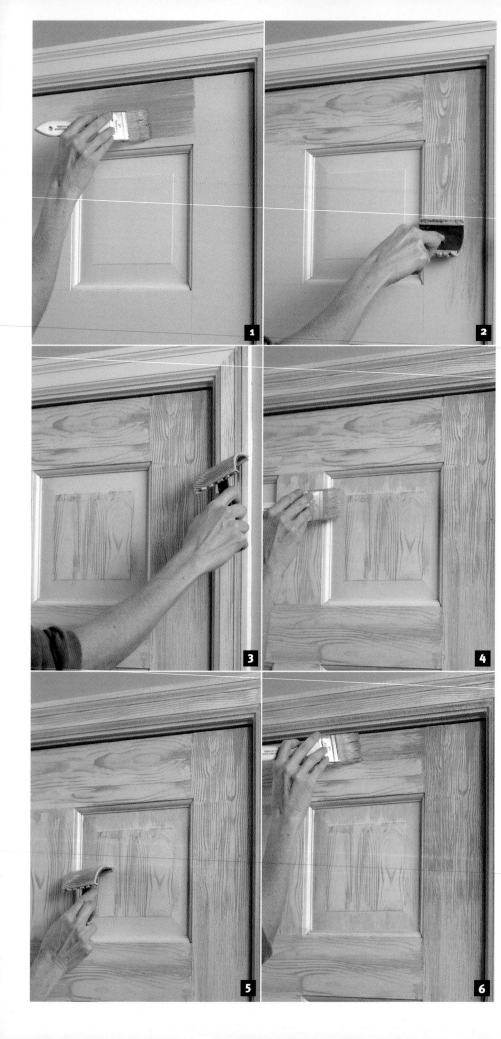

INSTRUCTIONS

If you are not planning to repaint your walls, tape around door molding with painter's tape. Use a trim brush to paint the door with the white base coat color. Paint two coats if necessary. Leave tape on; let dry overnight.

1

Mix 1 part light brown and 1 part blue-gray to 4 parts glaze medium in a plastic container. Apply to a small area using a 2-inch chip brush. You may find it is easier to work on one area at a time.

2

Drag the wood-graining tool over the area you've glazed, rocking it back and forth as you pull. Step back and review your work. The glaze will stay wet for some time, so if you are unhappy with the graining, simply pull the tool through the glaze again, varying how fast you rock it back and forth and where you start and stop on the tool. After you are happy with the results and while the glaze is still wet, lightly brush with a clean, dry chip brush in the direction of the grain to soften.

3

After brushing the glaze onto the door molding, use the comb edge of the tool to drag through the glaze. Most moldings have ridges and will respond better to fine combing to achieve grain. As you pull the tool across the surface, slightly waver your stroke for a more realistic result.

4

Lightly brush glaze into the corners of the panels. Wipe the brush onto a cloth to remove excess glaze when needed.

5

Use the comb edge of the tool to grain small corners and edges you cannot reach with the main section of the tool. Allow the door to dry.

6

Mix 1 part light brown to 2 parts blue-gray and brush lightly onto selected areas such as the top and bottom corners of the door and around the doorknob. Allow to dry.

7

Dip the 2-inch trowel into the white paint and skip it across the door surface, barely letting the trowel touch the door. Practice skipping the paint on a piece of scrap board or foam core before trying it on the door.

Continue this process until the door is completed.

8

Mix 1 part white paint to 4 parts glaze medium and brush lightly to soften areas. Remove tape; allow to dry.

TIP WORK WITH A CONTRASTING COLOR PALETTE AND VARY THE AMOUNT OF GLAZE YOU APPLY TO THE SURFACE FOR A DRAMATIC WORN LOOK.

faux venetian plaster

This faux Venetian plaster technique uses thin layers of paint to simulate the look of worn plaster. A trowel takes the place of a brush to apply layers of paint, further enhancing the aged look. For more dramatic results, choose colors of varying intensity. This finish works best when applied to smooth walls. Before you start, apply a base coat of white latex paint or primer if you wish. Try the technique in a dining room, den, or bath for a rich effect.

SKILL LEVEL Intermediate

TOOLS YOU'LL NEED

A

B

C

DARK BROWN, RUST, PALE GOLD, CREAMY YELLOW, AND OFF-WHITE SATIN FINISH LATEX PAINTS

DROP CLOTH

STIR STICKS

2 DISPOSABLE FOIL PANS (A)

6-INCH PLASTIC TROWEL (B)

LINT-FREE COTTON CLOTHS (C)

DARK BROWN, RUST, PALE GOLD, CREAMY YELLOW, AND OFF-WHITE LATEX PAINTS

INSTRUCTIONS

Mask areas that you wish to protect with painter's tape. Pour dark brown, rust, and pale gold into one foil pan. Pour pale gold, creamy yellow, and off-white into the other foil pan. Do not mix the colors.

Dip the trowel into dark brown. Beginning at the bottom of the wall, apply the paint about one-quarter of the way up the wall; wipe remaining paint off the trowel with a cotton cloth.

1

Dip the trowel into creamy yellow, then into off-white so that there are two colors on the trowel. The colors will mix as you dip your trowel into the pan. Starting near the top of the wall, apply the paint with horizontal and vertical strokes as you move down the wall.

2

Continue picking up two colors at a time. Using progressively darker colors and working toward the bottom of the wall, connect the color at the top to the dark brown section.

3

Blend the dark brown into the lighter colors.

4

After you have applied color to the entire wall, step back and evaluate the effect. Add more tones and highlights as desired. Remove tape; allow to dry.

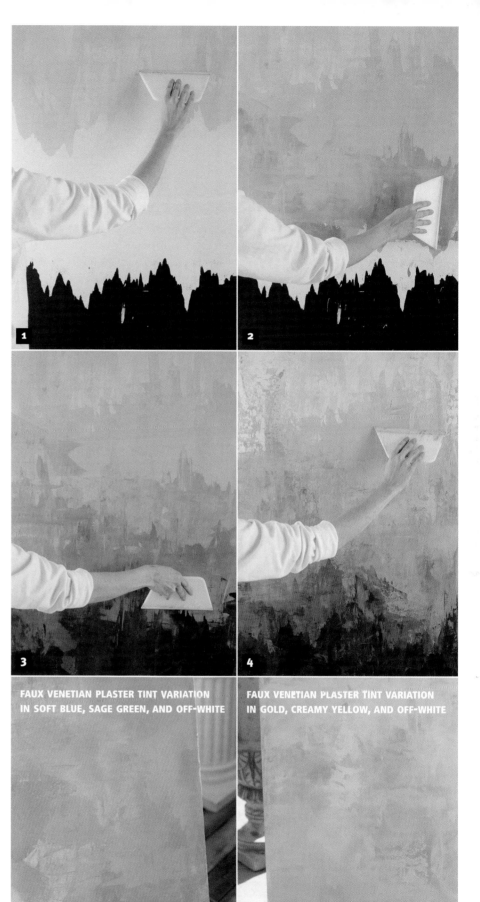

FAUX VENETIAN PLASTER TINT VARIATION IN SOFT BLUE, SAGE GREEN, AND OFF-WHITE

FAUX VENETIAN PLASTER TINT VARIATION IN GOLD, CREAMY YELLOW, AND OFF-WHITE

crumbled plaster

The tan cracked stucco finish is created using a specially formulated plaster trowelled directly onto the wall with crumbs thrown into the wet surface (see *page 190* for sources). The plaster is applied unevenly, and cracks occur in the areas where the plaster coat is heavier. The steps to this technique are not difficult or time-consuming, but you do need patience. Let each layer dry thoroughly before moving to the next step. This antique wall finish will complement a country French or Italian-inspired decor but also suits an urban-industrial look.

SKILL LEVEL Advanced

TOOLS YOU'LL NEED

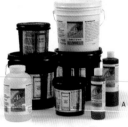

OFF-WHITE AQUABOND; EARTH BROWN AND AUTUMN BROWN AQUACOLOR; SANDSTONE, LIME SLAG, PLASTERTEX, AND AQUACREME (A) SEE RESOURCES PAGE 190

2-INCH LOW-TACK PAINTER'S TAPE

DROP CLOTH, WATERPROOF

STIR STICKS

PAINT TRAY

STANDARD ROLLER FRAME WITH 9-INCH ROLLER COVER

2-INCH TAPERED TRIM BRUSH

WATER

MINI ROLLER FRAME WITH 6-INCH FABRIC ROLLER COVER (B)

STAINLESS-STEEL TROWEL

LINT-FREE COTTON CLOTHS

RUBBER GLOVES

4-INCH PLASTIC TROWEL

220-GRIT SANDPAPER

SPRAY BOTTLE WITH WATER

LARGE BRUSH

INSTRUCTIONS

Mask ceilings, baseboards, and trim with painter's tape. Paint the entire wall in the Off-White AquaBond using a standard paint roller. Leave tape on; let dry overnight.

Create crumbs by mixing 4 cups of SandStone with ½ cup Lime Slag.

1

Dilute the SandStone with 10 to 20 percent water; then roll on a thin "scratch" coat with the mini fabric roller, covering the entire surface. Let dry.

Lightly scrape the dried SandStone with the stainless-steel trowel to knock off any roughness. Wipe dust off with a cotton cloth. Roll a thin, even coat of PlasterTex onto the surface using the fabric roller.

2

Allow to set 5 to 10 minutes and then compress it into the substrate with a stainless-steel trowel. Let dry for at least 1 hour. Randomly add more PlasterTex to the surface using the trowel; skip around over the surface and build up a heavier coat in some areas.

3

Put on rubber gloves. While the plaster is still wet, apply crumbs by either throwing them into the wet surface or by placing them on a plastic trowel and pressing them in.

4

Knock down the materials with a stainless steel-trowel but do not smooth the crumbs and texture out completely; leave some areas with a heavier and more crumbly coating than others.

Cracks will occur in the more heavily coated areas. Let dry overnight.

5

Knock off any loose crumbs or plaster and lightly sand the surface with sandpaper. Remove sanding dust with a cloth.

Make a warm brown glaze with 2 cups AquaCreme, 4 tablespoons of Earth Brown AquaColor, and 4 teaspoons of Autumn Brown AquaColor.

6

Mist the surface with a thin film of water.

7

Apply a coat of the warm brown glaze to the surface using a large brush, working it into all the cracks and crevices.

8

Lightly rub with a dry cotton cloth to remove excess glaze.

9

Remove tape; allow to dry.

TIP THIS IS A MESSY TECHNIQUE. MASK OFF SURFACES WITH LOW-TACK PAINTER'S TAPE AND PROTECT YOUR FLOOR WITH A WATERPROOF DROP CLOTH.

venetianplaster

Venetian plaster has been used for centuries to create textured and elegant interiors. The process involves applying thin layers of plaster over a base coat of paint or primer, using a trowel. After the plaster has dried, the surface is burnished for a polished effect and then sealed with paste wax. Create an overall even finish, as in the bedroom *below*, by keeping strokes and pressure consistent. For a more irregular surface, vary your strokes, pressure, and colors. As you add layers, the plaster will dry faster. Avoid overworking areas because this can lead to making small scratches in the drying plaster. Wipe the blade often to avoid getting dried plaster in the fresh plaster. Practice the procedure on a scrap board first to make sure you get the color you want.

SKILL LEVEL Intermediate

TOOLS YOU'LL NEED

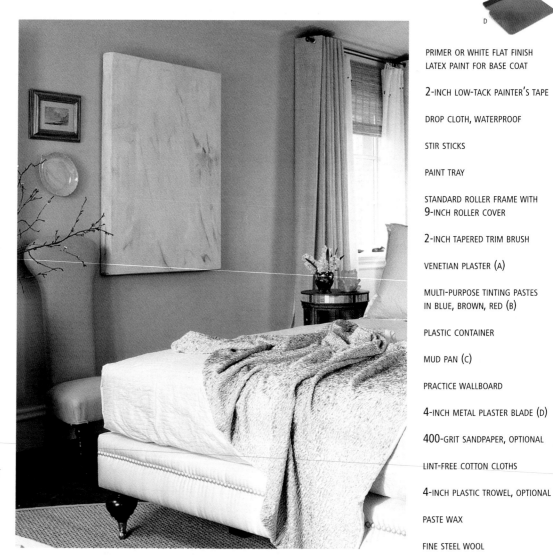

WHITE PRIMER OR LATEX PAINT

PRIMER OR WHITE FLAT FINISH LATEX PAINT FOR BASE COAT

2-INCH LOW-TACK PAINTER'S TAPE

DROP CLOTH, WATERPROOF

STIR STICKS

PAINT TRAY

STANDARD ROLLER FRAME WITH 9-INCH ROLLER COVER

2-INCH TAPERED TRIM BRUSH

VENETIAN PLASTER (A)

MULTI-PURPOSE TINTING PASTES IN BLUE, BROWN, RED (B)

PLASTIC CONTAINER

MUD PAN (C)

PRACTICE WALLBOARD

4-INCH METAL PLASTER BLADE (D)

400-GRIT SANDPAPER, OPTIONAL

LINT-FREE COTTON CLOTHS

4-INCH PLASTIC TROWEL, OPTIONAL

PASTE WAX

FINE STEEL WOOL

INSTRUCTIONS

Mask ceiling, baseboards, and trim with painter's tape. The surface should be clean, dry, and free of dust. Prime or paint the surface using white paint. Apply two coats if necessary. Leave tape on; let dry overnight.

Mix plaster with tinting pastes in a plastic container. Mix 8 drops of blue to 2 drops each of red and brown per gallon of plaster. Add tints gradually to obtain the desired color. The plaster will dry lighter, so test on a practice board and allow to dry completely to ensure the right color. Put a portion of the plaster into a mud pan.

1

Use a 4-inch metal plaster blade and practice applying plaster onto a piece of scrap wallboard. Wipe excess plaster off the blade using the angled sides of the mud pan. When you are ready, start in an upper corner and work down and across the wall. Place a thin strip of plaster on the rim of the blade. Deposit all the material from the blade onto the wall in one pass. Make another light pass over the same area to remove excess material and redistribute it further along the wall. This will leave only a thin, smooth coat of plaster. Repeat to cover the wall. Allow to dry approximately 15 minutes.

2

Between coats, smooth the surface with 400-grit sandpaper or a clean blade. Apply at least two more thin coats of plaster. Allow to dry before applying the next coat.

3

For a highly polished finish, burnish the surface 4 to 6 hours after the final

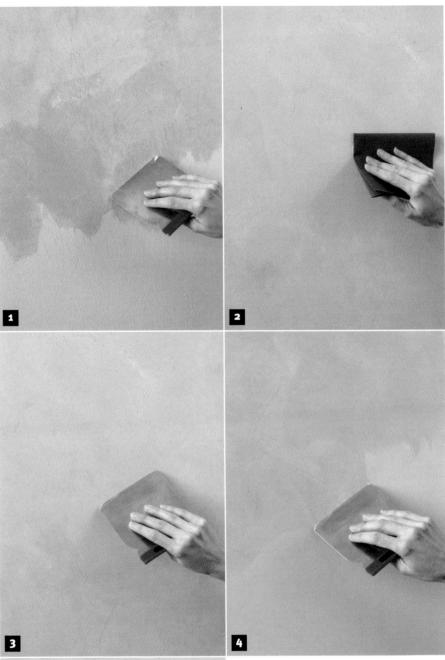

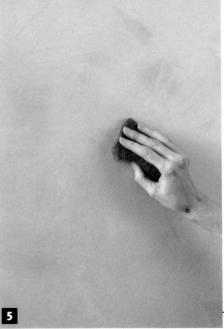

plaster coat. To burnish, lightly rub the surface with a clean blade; on light colors, use a plastic trowel to avoid dark streaks.

4

Apply paste wax with a clean blade to seal the surface and enhance the color.

5

Once the wax has cured, polish the surface with a clean blade, cloth, or fine steel wool. Use a plastic trowel on lighter colors to avoid leaving dark streaks. Remove tape; allow to dry.

32

colorwash

Color washing provides an informal, textured look using translucent layers of color. Terra-cotta paint applied over an off-white base coat color in a simple crisscross motion gives walls old-world charm. A trimming brush is used to apply the glaze, but other tools such as a sea sponge and soft cloth can also be used. The sea sponge will increase the textured look, while the cloth will soften or diffuse the color. A versatile technique, color washing provides the perfect textured background to combine with other paint finishes such as striping, blocks, stenciling, and stamping.

SKILL LEVEL Intermediate

TOOLS YOU'LL NEED

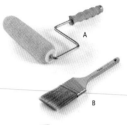

OFF-WHITE SATIN FINISH LATEX PAINT FOR BASE COAT; TERRA-COTTA SATIN FINISH LATEX PAINT FOR GLAZE COAT

2-INCH LOW-TACK PAINTER'S TAPE

DROP CLOTH

STIR STICKS

PAINT TRAY

STANDARD ROLLER FRAME WITH 9-INCH ROLLER COVER (A)

2-INCH TAPERED TRIM BRUSH (B)

GLAZE MEDIUM (C)

PLASTIC CONTAINER WITH PRINTED MEASUREMENTS

OFF-WHITE AND TERRA-COTTA LATEX PAINTS

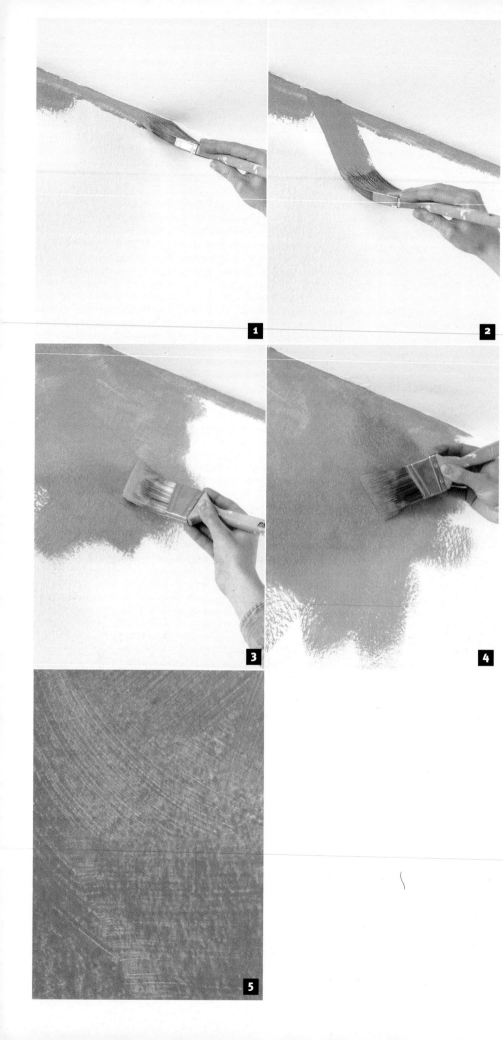

INSTRUCTIONS

Mask baseboards and trim with painter's tape. Paint the entire wall in the off-white base coat color. Paint two coats if necessary. Leave tape on; let dry overnight.

Mix 4 parts glaze to 1 part paint in a plastic container. If the mixture is drying too quickly or seems heavy, add more glaze. Mix well.

1

Starting with one wall, use a 2-inch trim brush to begin cutting in the glaze starting at the ceiling line and working down. Cut a straight line in the corners also.

2

Working quickly, crosshatch through the glaze so the straight line does not remain. Trim along the edges and moldings as usual, but brush out the trimming lines using a crosshatch motion.

3 **4**

Continue making Xs as you crosshatch the glaze. Try to complete one wall without drying lines appearing.

5

Remove all tape; allow to dry.

TIP TRY TO COMPLETE AN ENTIRE WALL WITHOUT STOPPING. IF YOU MUST STOP, FEATHER OUT THE EDGES OF THE PAINTED AREAS. WHEN YOU RESUME PAINTING, OVERLAP THE GLAZE AS LITTLE AS POSSIBLE TO AVOID DARKER AREAS ON THE WALL. OR, DIVIDE THE WALL INTO VERTICAL PANELS AND TAPE OFF USING PAINTER'S TAPE. COLOR WASH EVERY OTHER PANEL. REMOVE THE TAPE, THEN TAPE OFF AND COLOR WASH REMAINING PANELS.

colorwashvariations

1 The walls and ceiling in this dressing room were painted in a lavender base coat then washed in taupe for a vintage look. The wall color was inspired by a lavender-and-taupe table skirt (not shown). Fabrics are often used as a starting point when selecting paint colors.

2 White chair-rail molding separates two color washes of contrasting intensity. Light green paint covers the entire wall, but above the chair rail a mixture of 4 parts glaze to 1 part paint is used.

Below the chair rail the mixture is 1 part glaze to 1 part paint.

3 Color washing provides a subtle background that combines easily with other techniques, such as stripes. In this charming bedroom, two blue glazes are applied over a white base coat in alternating 8-inch stripes.

blendedcolorwash

Color washing is the ideal technique to use on walls with imperfections, such as old plaster walls, because the layered paint treatment turns the wall's flaws into a source of dimension and character. The effect shown *below* is created by blending six paint colors, working from the lightest to the darkest shade. Cheesecloth, or lightweight cotton gauze, is used to blend the colors to avoid removing too much glaze. The same technique applied to smooth walls will give a similar appearance of texture.

SKILL LEVEL Intermediate

TOOLS YOU'LL NEED

A

B

C

D

LIGHT GREEN SEMIGLOSS FINISH LATEX PAINT FOR BASE COAT; 5 GREENISH-BLUE SHADES FROM LIGHTEST TO DARKEST, SEMIGLOSS FINISH LATEX PAINTS FOR GLAZE COATS

2-INCH LOW-TACK PAINTER'S TAPE

DROP CLOTH

STIR STICKS

PAINT TRAY

STANDARD ROLLER FRAME WITH 9-INCH ROLLER COVER

2-INCH TAPERED TRIM BRUSH

GLAZE MEDIUM (A)

PLASTIC CONTAINER WITH PRINTED MEASUREMENTS

6 SMALL DISPOSABLE ALUMINUM PANS (B)

PAINTBRUSH

CHEESECLOTHS (C)

BRUSH WITH BADGER-HAIR BRISTLES (D)

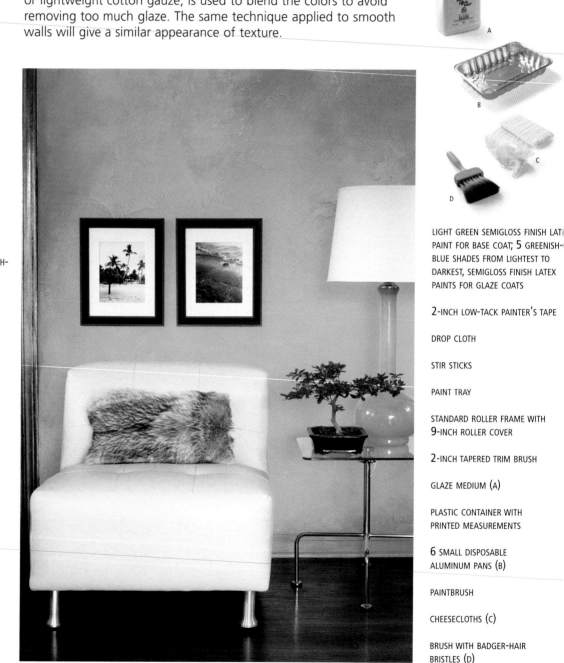

LIGHT GREEN AND 5 GREENISH-BLUE SHADES LATEX PAINTS

INSTRUCTIONS

Mask ceiling, baseboards, and trim with painter's tape.

1

Paint the entire wall in the light green base coat color. Paint two coats if necessary. Leave tape on; let dry overnight.

2

Mix 4 parts glaze to 1 part paint for each glaze coat color in a plastic container. Pour tinted glazes into aluminum pans. Using a paintbrush, randomly apply various color glazes to the wall, working in small areas.

3

Start with the darkest hue in the upper left corner then add a random coating of a medium-hue tinted glaze along the edges of the dark. End with the lightest tinted glaze in the center of the wall.

4

While the paint is still wet, blot the area with cheesecloth, blending the colors into the base coat. When the cloth gets too heavy, fold it over or use a new one. You will need to change cloths often. Blotting the paint will expand your brushed-on design.

5

Before the paint dries, soften any brush or blotting marks with a badger-hair bristle brush. Be sure to clean and dry the brush before using it again. Repeat from each corner working your way to the center until you reach the desired results; let dry. If the design appears too light, add more tinted glaze in the appropriate areas. Remove tape; allow to dry.

TIPS START WITH A BASE COAT THAT IS LIGHT AND REFLECTIVE. ALWAYS ADD DARKER COLORS TO LIGHTER COLORS.

WORK THE DARKEST HUES INTO THE CORNERS TO CREATE A MORE AUTHENTIC AGED APPEARANCE.

graduatedcolorwash

The watercolor wash is achieved by combining several shades of green and blue glazes and applying them with long horizontal brushstrokes. Before applying paint to your wall, experiment on a practice board. This will allow you to become comfortable with the technique and provide you with a sample to tack onto your wall. This technique works best on walls without windows and doors. Try the finish on just one wall for an eye-catching focal point.

SKILL LEVEL Intermediate

TOOLS YOU'LL NEED

WHITE SEMIGLOSS LATEX PAINT FOR BASE COAT; DARK GREEN, LIGHT BLUE, AND LIGHTER BLUE SEMIGLOSS LATEX PAINTS FOR GLAZE COAT

2-INCH LOW-TACK PAINTER'S TAPE

DROP CLOTH

STIR STICKS

PAINT TRAY

STANDARD ROLLER FRAME WITH 9-INCH ROLLER COVER

2-INCH TAPERED TRIM BRUSH

LEVEL WITH PRINTED RULER (A)

LIGHT BLUE COLORED PENCIL

GLAZE MEDIUM (B)

3 PLASTIC CONTAINERS WITH PRINTED MEASUREMENTS

3- TO 4-INCH GOOD-QUALITY PAINTBRUSH (C)

WHITE, DARK GREEN, LIGHT BLUE, AND LIGHTER BLUE LATEX PAINTS

INSTRUCTIONS

Mask ceiling, baseboards, and trim with painter's tape. Paint the entire wall in the white base coat. Paint two coats if necessary. Leave tape on; let dry overnight.

1

Using a level with printed ruler and a blue pencil, mark horizontal lines 2 feet and 4 feet up from the baseboard.

2

Mix three separate glazes using each of the remaining three paint colors in the three plastic containers, using 1 part paint to 3 parts glaze. Using a good-quality paintbrush, brush dark green glaze along the bottom of the wall near the baseboard, making the strokes as long as possible. Work 2 feet up the wall in this manner.

3

Without washing the brush, dip it into the darker blue glaze and begin brushing the glaze onto the wall with long horizontal strokes, blending the blue and green together. Continue 2 feet up the wall with the blue glaze. The green will continue to mix with the blue as it comes off the brush.

4

Dip the brush into the lighter blue glaze and brush it onto the remainder of the wall with long horizontal strokes, blending the blues.

Work on one wall at a time, taping off adjoining walls to keep them clean. Allow the painted walls to dry before working on adjoining walls.

Continue until all walls are completed. Remove tape; allow to dry.

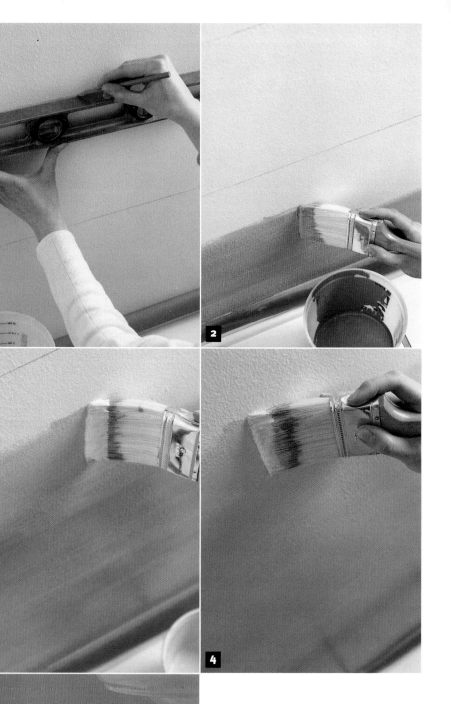

TIPS THIS TECHNIQUE NEEDS TO BE DONE QUICKLY FOR THE BEST RESULTS.

TO AVOID BUYING TWO SHADES OF BLUE PAINT, BUY THE DARKER BLUE AND ADD A LITTLE WHITE PAINT TO LIGHTEN.

whitewashing

Whitewashing, also referred to as pickling or liming, is a simple technique that uses paint diluted with water to reveal some of the natural wood grain underneath. Whitewashing can be used on any raw wood surface. When applying the paint, it's best to move quickly and always wash with the grain of the wood. It's a messy technique because of the runny wash mixture. Take extra care in protecting flooring and other surfaces. White paint is usually the color of choice for a charming cottage or country style, but pastel colors are also popular. For the girl's room *below*, whitewashed beaded board is complemented by a shelf hand-painted with scallops.

SKILL LEVEL Beginner

TOOLS YOU'LL NEED

A

B

C

WHITE SEMIGLOSS FINISH LATEX PAINT

DROP CLOTH, WATERPROOF (A)

WATER

PLASTIC CONTAINER WITH PRINTED MEASUREMENTS

STIR STICK

2-INCH TAPERED TRIM BRUSH (B)

LINT-FREE COTTON CLOTHS, OPTIONAL (C)

WHITE LATEX PAINT

INSTRUCTIONS

Mask baseboards and trim with painter's tape. Mix 1 part white paint with 1 part water. Stir well.

1

Using a 2-inch tapered trim brush, begin painting from the top to the bottom, moving quickly. Start in a corner, cutting in the edge and moving out. Try not to get any of the wash on the adjoining wall. If you do get wash on an adjoining wall, wipe it off with a damp cloth and feather off the edges with a paintbrush.

2

Finish one wall before starting the next. If the whitewashing process stops before a wall is finished, the ending and starting points will be obvious. If you like, use a cloth to remove some of the paint, revealing more of the natural wood grain.

3

Repeat with another coat if desired. Allow the first coat to dry completely before adding another one.

4

Remove tape; allow to dry.

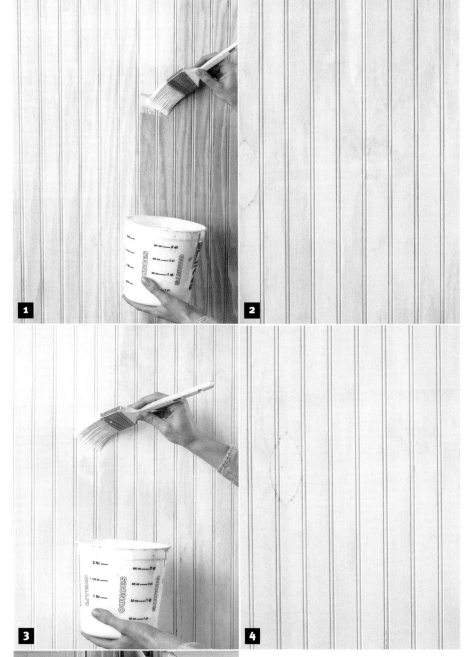

ALSO TRY WHITEWASHING ON FLOORS. TAPE OFF DIAMONDS AS FOR WALLS (PAGE 42).

TIPS ALWAYS MAKE SURE THE SURFACE IS SANDED AND WIPED CLEAN PRIOR TO PAINTING SO THE DILUTED PAINT WILL ADHERE TO THE WALL.

TAPING OFF WALLS IS NOT RECOMMENDED FOR THIS TECHNIQUE BECAUSE THE RUNNY WASH MAY BLEED UNDER THE TAPE AND DRY, LEAVING OBVIOUS LINES.

alloverstencil

An allover damask stencil suggests the look of elaborate wallpaper. The tone-on-tone damask pattern is laid between stripes created by a vertically stenciled border. For a more distressed, aged look, use random pressure to allow the color to fade away in places as you stencil. This timeless, elegant style works well in a room with dark, rich furnishings and accessories.

SKILL LEVEL Advanced

TOOLS YOU'LL NEED

OFF-WHITE, DEEP GOLD, AND TERRA-COTTA LATEX PAINTS

OFF-WHITE SATIN FINISH LATEX PAINT FOR BASE COAT; DEEP GOLD AND TERRA COTTA SATIN FINISH LATEX PAINTS FOR GLAZE COATS

2-INCH LOW-TACK PAINTER'S TAPE

DROP CLOTH

STIR STICK

PAINT TRAY

STANDARD ROLLER FRAME WITH 9-INCH ROLLER COVER

2-INCH TAPERED TRIM BRUSH

2 PLASTIC CONTAINERS WITH PRINTED MEASUREMENTS

GLAZE MEDIUM (A)

LINT-FREE COTTON CLOTHS

LEVEL WITH PRINTED RULER

BROWN COLORED PENCIL

STENCILS, SEE RESOURCES PAGE 191

FOAM BRUSH

SEA SPONGE (B)

LARGE STENCIL BRUSH (C)

STENCIL SPRAY ADHESIVE (D)

INSTRUCTIONS

Mask ceiling, baseboards, and trim with painter's tape. Paint the entire wall in the off-white base coat color. Paint two coats if necessary. Leave tape on; let dry overnight.

Mix 3 parts glaze to 1 part deep gold paint in a plastic container. Roll on the glaze and wipe off with a clean cotton cloth to create a subtle texture.

1

Using the stencil widths as your guide, determine the layout of the stripes and the width of the pattern in between. Use a level to measure and mark off plumb guidelines. Draw light lines with a colored pencil and level.

2

Tape off the areas for the border stripes and apply a second layer of glaze to deepen the tone using a foam brush. Immediately after applying the glaze, soften the glazed stripe with a damp sea sponge.

Allow to dry. Remove the tape around the borders.

3

Add terra-cotta paint to the glaze mixture to deepen the color. Use the new glaze to stencil the stripe/border design. Use a stencil spray adhesive and painter's tape to hold the stencil in position. Stencil the all-over damask pattern in between using the same color.

4

When the entire wall is completed, remove tape; allow to dry.

TIP WHEN STENCILING WITH GLAZE, BE SURE TO REMOVE EXCESS PAINT BY WIPING THE BRUSH ON ABSORBENT PAPER TOWELS. THIS PREVENTS THE GLAZE FROM LEAKING UNDER THE STENCILS.

alloverstencilvariations

1 The inspiration for this allover stencil pattern was the apron of an intricately embroidered Ukrainian folk art costume. Photos of the apron were photocopied and enlarged. The diamondlike motif was broken down into five stencils that are applied in eight subtle colors.

2 Damask-motif stencils in a muted green color give an elegant air to a high-traffic entryway. Bands of solid green above the wainscoting and at the top of the wall (not shown) add a finishing touch.

3 The stencil treatment in this bath mimics the look of a delicate wallpaper pattern. The stencil is applied with a tinted glaze, then gently rubbed with a cheesecloth to achieve an aged effect. The advantage of painting as opposed to wallpapering is that you can customize the color to achieve the exact shade you want for the room.

flower&vinestencil

A stenciled white flowery border dances across bright lavender walls in the girl's room *below*. A sheer curtain with appliquéd flowers and vines inspired the charming border. The flowers were hand-drawn, using the window covering as a guide, and then enlarged to have more impact at the ceiling line. Look for stencil plastic at arts and crafts stores. Translucent plastic is easiest to use: simply lay it over the pattern and trace with a fine-tip marker. If you use an opaque stencil material such as opaque stencil board or poster board, you'll need to use carbon paper or graph paper to transfer the pattern.

SKILL LEVEL Intermediate

TOOLS YOU'LL NEED

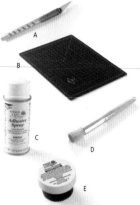

BRIGHT LAVENDER SATIN FINISH LATEX PAINT FOR BASE COAT

2-INCH LOW-TACK PAINTER'S TAPE

DROP CLOTH

STIR STICK

PAINT TRAY

STANDARD ROLLER FRAME WITH 9-INCH ROLLER COVER

2-INCH TAPERED TRIM BRUSH

STENCIL PATTERN, PAGE 182

STENCIL PLASTIC

GRAPHITE OR CARBON PAPER

FINE-TIP MARKER

CRAFTS KNIFE WITH EXTRA BLADES (A)

SELF-HEALING CUTTING MAT (B)

STENCIL SPRAY ADHESIVE (C)

MEDIUM-SIZED STENCILING BRUSH (D)

WHITE STENCIL PAINT (E)

PAPER TOWELS OR COTTON CLOTHS

BRIGHT LAVENDER LATEX PAINT

INSTRUCTIONS

Mask ceiling, baseboards, and trim
with painter's tape. Paint the entire
wall in the lavender base coat color.
Paint two coats if necessary. Remove
tape; let dry overnight.

Use a photocopier to enlarge the
pattern on page 182 to the desired size.

1

When you are satisfied with the size of
the design, transfer it to stencil plastic.
If the material isn't large enough, tape
two pieces together.

2

Cut out the stencil design using a crafts
knife and self-healing cutting mat. Use
a new blade for a clean, sharp line and
change blades as needed.

3

Roll the stencil back onto itself to
trace part of the pattern for registration
marks to help position the stencil.

4

Spray the back of the stencil with
spray adhesive. Add tape if necessary.
Place the stencil just below the ceiling.

5

Dip the medium-size stenciling brush
into a small amount of white stencil
paint and blot excess paint onto a paper
towel or cloth. Use a gentle circular or
light tapping motion to fill in the stencil.

6

Carefully lift off the stencil. Line up
the registration pattern and continue
stenciling across the wall.

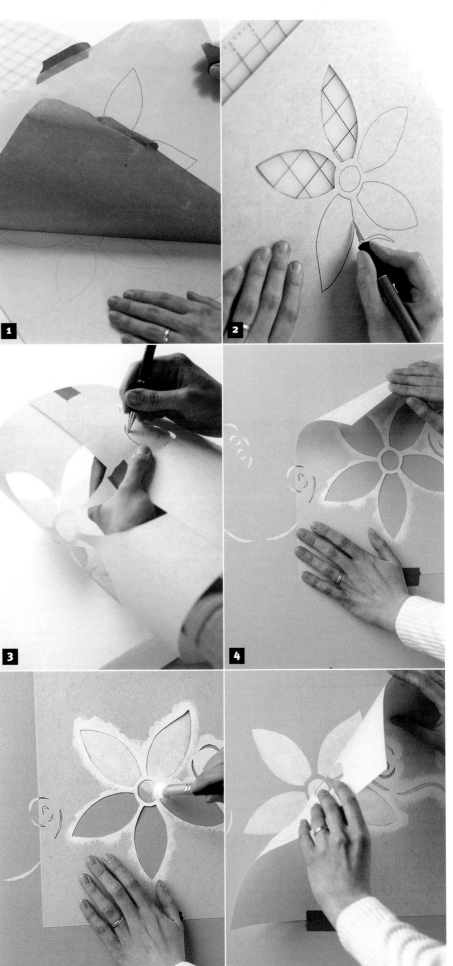

simple curved stencil

The curves of an iron chandelier provided the inspiration for a simple stencil motif in the dining room *below*. The stencil connects the motif to the architecture at door height and visually substitutes for a chair rail lower on the wall. Painting this simple motif in gold metallic paint catches the light and enhances the warmth and elegance of the red walls. The same motif would also work as an allover stencil design in a stylish bath.

SKILL LEVEL Beginner

TOOLS YOU'LL NEED

RED SATIN FINISH LATEX PAINT FOR BASE COAT

2-INCH LOW-TACK PAINTER'S TAPE

DROP CLOTH

STIR STICK

PAINT TRAY

STANDARD ROLLER FRAME WITH 9-INCH ROLLER COVER

2-INCH TAPERED TRIM BRUSH

STENCIL PATTERN, PAGE 182

STENCIL PLASTIC

FINE-TIP MARKER

GRAPHITE OR CARBON PAPER

CRAFTS KNIFE (A)

SELF-HEALING CUTTING MAT (B)

WOODEN YARDSTICK

LEVEL

GOLD COLORED PENCIL

STENCIL SPRAY ADHESIVE

SMALL STENCIL BRUSH (C)

GOLD-TONE METALLIC OIL-BASED STENCIL PAINT

LINT-FREE COTTON CLOTHS, OPTIONAL

RED LATEX PAINT

INSTRUCTIONS

Mask ceiling, baseboards, and trim with painter's tape. Paint the entire wall in the red base coat color. Paint two coats if necessary. Remove tape; let dry overnight.

Use a photocopier to enlarge the pattern on page 182 to the desired size. When you are satisfied with the size of the design, transfer it to stencil material. If you are using an opaque stencil material, use graph paper or carbon paper to transfer the pattern to opaque stencil board or poster board. If you are using translucent stencil plastic, place the pattern underneath the stencil plastic and trace with a fine-tip marker.

Cut out the stencil design with a crafts knife on a self-healing cutting mat. Use a new blade and change the blade as soon as it begins to dull.

1
Determine the height of the borders, then level the yardstick and tape it in place for one row. For the borders shown one row is positioned at chair-rail height, and the other row is slightly below the height of the doorway.

2
Use the level straightedge as a guide for positioning the stencil across the wall. Spray the back of the stencil with spray adhesive to hold it in place. Add tape if necessary. Apply paint in a swirling motion by using a small stencil brush.

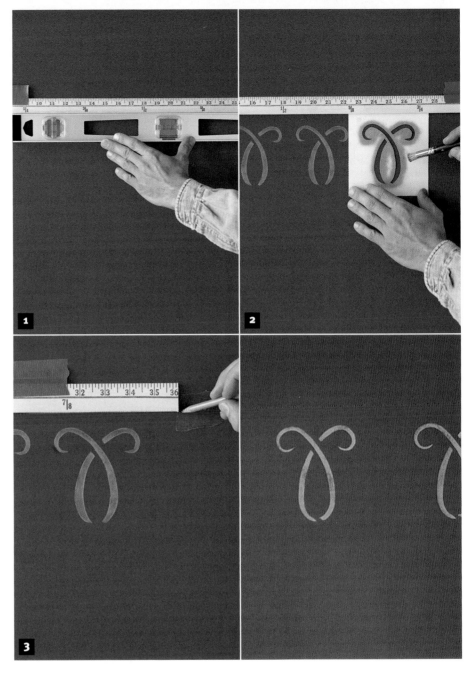

3
When you reach the end of the yardstick, place a piece of tape and mark it with the pencil. Use this point to extend and level the yardstick across the wall.

4
Continue stenciling until completed. Allow to dry.

TIP IF YOU ARE USING A SMALL JAR OF SOLID OIL-BASED STENCIL PAINT, APPLY THE PAINT IN A SWIRLING MOTION. IF YOU ARE STENCILING WITH LIQUID LATEX PAINT, BLOT THE BRUSH ON SCRAP PAPER OR A CLEAN CLOTH AND APPLY WITH A STIPPLING, TAPPING MOTION.

rosettestencil

In a spacious room, the orderly, well-spaced placement of this large-scale Asian-inspired rosette stencil creates a quiet, contemplative mood. In a small space, such as a powder room, the stencil is stunningly dramatic. Paint the rosettes over a Tuscan-plaster finish to give the walls complexity and depth (or, if you prefer, paper the walls with a faux-finish wallcovering and apply the stencil to the wallpaper). The rosettes are spaced 30 inches apart in the room *opposite*, but measure your wall's height and width and space the rosettes to suit your room's dimensions and your taste.

SKILL LEVEL Intermediate

TOOLS YOU'LL NEED

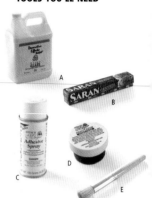

LIGHT GOLDEN TAN SATIN FINISH LATEX PAINT FOR BASE COAT; BROWNISH GOLD, DARK GOLDEN TAN, AND YELLOWISH GOLD SATIN FINISH LATEX PAINTS FOR GLAZE

2-INCH LOW-TACK PAINTER'S TAPE

DROP CLOTH

STIR STICKS

PAINT TRAY

STANDARD ROLLER FRAME WITH 9-INCH ROLLER COVER

2-INCH TAPERED TRIM BRUSH

3 PLASTIC CONTAINERS WITH PRINTED MEASUREMENTS

GLAZE MEDIUM (A)

PLASTIC WRAP (B)

LEVEL WITH PRINTED RULER

BROWN COLORED PENCIL

ROSETTE STENCIL, SEE RESOURCES PAGE 191

STENCIL SPRAY ADHESIVE (C)

BLACK CHERRY STENCIL PAINT (D)

LARGE STENCIL BRUSH (E)

LIGHT GOLDEN TAN, BROWNISH GOLD, DARK GOLDEN TAN, AND YELLOWISH GOLD LATEX PAINTS

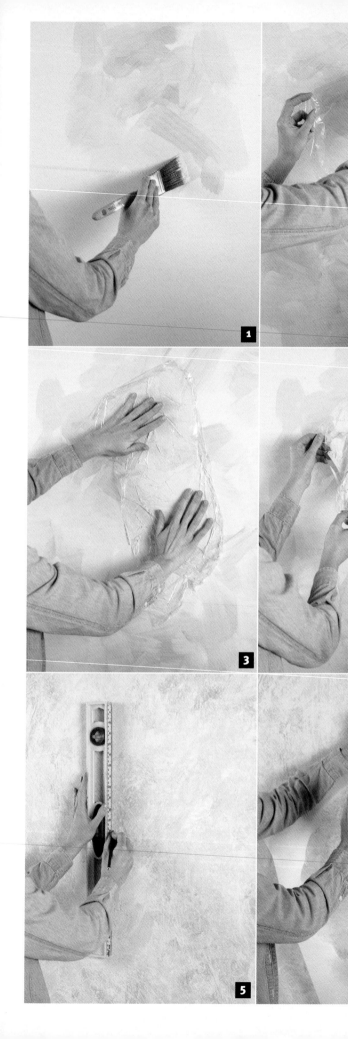

INSTRUCTIONS

Mask ceiling, baseboards, and trim with painter's tape. Paint the entire wall in the light golden tan base coat color. Paint two coats if necessary. Leave tape on; let dry overnight.

Mix the three glazes separately in plastic containers, each in a ratio of 4 parts glaze to 1 part paint.

1

Apply the glazes to the wall, trimming in the corners and ceiling lines as you go. Using a paintbrush, randomly apply the three glazes to the wall, working in an area about 4 feet by 4 feet. Keep the areas organic with uneven edges and irregular shapes.

2

After you complete the area, tear off a piece of plastic wrap approximately 2 feet long and quickly apply the plastic to the newly glazed areas, smoothing it down with the palm of your hand.

3

Do not let your fingertips drag along the plastic, although stationary fingertip pressure points are fine. As you texture with the plastic wrap, keep in mind that an overlap in color is desirable.

4

Lift the plastic off the wall and reapply it to an adjacent area. Repeat the smoothing and lifting procedure until you have textured the 4-foot-square area. Discard the plastic wrap after five uses and tear off a new sheet. Continue brushing on glazes and texturing with the plastic wrap until the wall is completed. Try to complete the entire wall before the glaze dries.

5

The rosettes shown are staggered 30 inches apart from center to center horizontally and vertically. Measure and mark the wall with

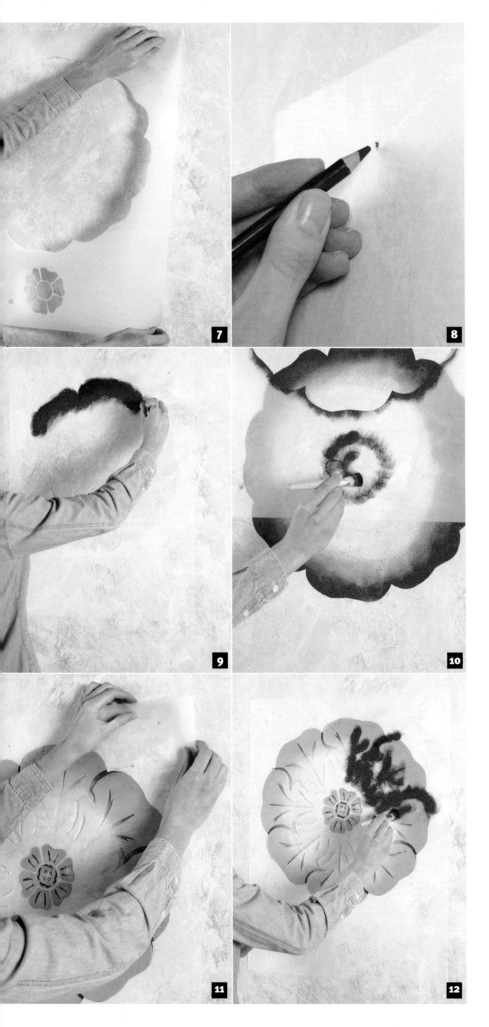

small dots to indicate placement of the center of the stencil. Start every other row 30 inches from the corner and the rows in between 15 inches from the corner.

6
Spray the first stencil overlay with stencil spray adhesive.

7
Apply the first overlay to the wall, centering it on the measurement mark. Use painter's tape to hold the stencil in place if needed.

8
Use a colored pencil to lightly mark the registration marks of the first overlay.

9
Swirl the large stencil brush into the black cherry paint and apply it to the first overlay in a swirling motion, starting at the edges and feathering as shown for a gradation in color. Do not stencil in a solid fashion.

Line up the registration marks of the second overlay. This one is connected to the bottom of the first overlay. Cut them apart if desired.

10
Stencil the second overlay using the same swirling motion.

11
Line up the third overlay using the registration marks as your guide.

12
Stencil the third and final overlay to complete the first rosette. Repeat the process until you have completed all the rosettes.

TIP ALWAYS USE A CLEAN PIECE OF PLASTIC WRAP WHEN YOU ARE WORKING NEXT TO THE CEILING LINE TO KEEP IT PAINT-FREE.

lacystencil

Three delicate lacy patterns stenciled along the upper wall and ceiling take the place of crown molding in the bedroom *below* and *opposite*. Off-white and golden tones play into the subtle feminine decor. Before you begin a project like this, measure the room and lay out the design according to the size of your stencils. To ensure that the stencil joints match up, begin in the most visible corner and work out from there. For a finishing touch, glue crystal beads to the stencil points to give the wall treatment dimension and added sparkle.

SKILL LEVEL Advanced

TOOLS YOU'LL NEED

WARM TAN SATIN FINISH LATEX PAIN
FOR BASE COAT; OFF-WHITE SATIN
FINISH LATEX PAINT FOR STENCIL;
GOLDEN SATIN FINISH LATEX PAINT
FOR GLAZE COAT

2-INCH LOW-TACK PAINTER'S TAPE

DROP CLOTH

STIR STICKS

PAINT TRAY

STANDARD ROLLER FRAME WITH
9-INCH ROLLER COVER

2-INCH TAPERED TRIM BRUSH

METAL YARDSTICK

GRAPHITE PENCIL

VICTORIAN FRIEZE STENCIL,
SEE RESOURCES PAGE 191

SMALL ITALIAN MEDALLION STENCIL,
SEE RESOURCES PAGE 191

LARGE STIPPLE BRUSH

SCRAP FOAMCORE AND PAPER

FLOWER CHAIN STENCIL, SEE
RESOURCES PAGE 191

GLAZE MEDIUM

PLASTIC CONTAINER WITH
PRINTED MEASUREMENTS

MINI ROLLER FRAME WITH
4-INCH ROLLER COVER

LINT-FREE COTTON CLOTHS

CRAFTS GLUE, OPTIONAL

CRYSTAL BEADS, OPTIONAL

WARM TAN, OFF-WHITE,
AND GOLDEN LATEX PAINTS

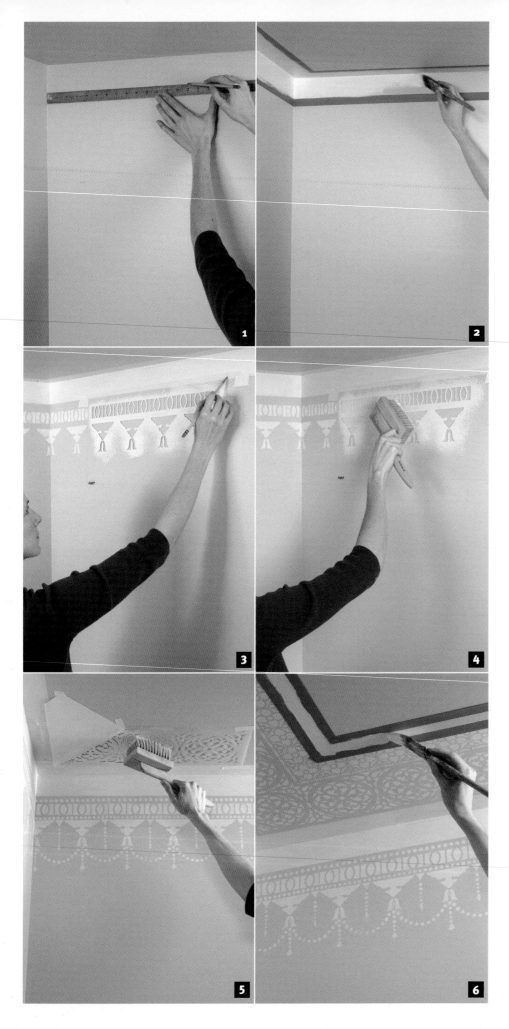

INSTRUCTIONS

Mask baseboards and trim with painter's tape. Paint the walls and ceiling in the warm tan base coat color. Paint two coats if necessary. Leave tape on; let dry overnight.

1

With a metal yardstick and pencil, mark off a 2-inch band around the top of the wall and another 2-inch band on the ceiling. Tape off the outer edges with painter's tape. Burnish the edge of the tape with your fingernail to ensure a sharp edge when you pull the tape off.

2

Brush on off-white paint with the 2-inch trim brush. Apply two coats if needed; allow to dry. Remove the tape. Use this band as a guide to position the Victorian Frieze stencil on the wall and the Italian Medallion on the ceiling.

3

When the stencil is taped in position, put a pencil mark in the hole of the stencil for the next placement. If you are moving left to right, mark only the right hole and vice versa.

4

Dip the stipple brush into the off-white paint and tap onto a piece of foamcore to distribute the paint evenly onto your brush. Stipple the stencil using a quick dabbing motion.

5

Apply the Small Italian Medallion stencil by repeating the stenciling procedure in Step 4. In the corners of the ceiling, after you position the stencil, fold a piece of paper on a 45-degree angle and tape it over the stencil to create a mitered corner. Repeat in each corner. Let the paint dry.

Apply the Flower Chain stencil in the same manner using the Small Italian Medallion stencil as a guide. Allow to dry.

6

Mark off and tape a 1-inch band on the ceiling. This line should be square and straight, so it's critical to measure from the wall and not the edge of the Flower Chain stencil. Burnish the inside edges of the tape with your fingernail. Apply off-white paint with a trim brush. Allow to dry and remove tape.

This will be your guide for the final repetition of the Victorian Frieze stencil.

7

Apply the Victorian Frieze stencil to the ceiling by repeating the instructions in Step 4. You will need to use extra tape when working on the ceiling to hold your stencil in place. Allow paint to dry.

8

Mix 1 part golden paint to 5 parts glaze in a plastic container. Using a mini roller, roll glaze over one small area at a time.

9

Use a lint-free cotton cloth to lightly wipe off the glaze. Soften the edges to blend the working areas together. Continue glazing and blending down the wall.

10

Soften and blend with the stipple brush as you go.

11

Remove tape; allow to dry.

12

If you desire, glue crystal beads to every other stencil point.

TIP USING A LARGE STIPPLE BRUSH HELPS A JOB OF THIS SIZE GO MUCH MORE QUICKLY.

linenstripegingkoleafstencil

A combination of three popular techniques decorates this charming bedroom *below*: striping, stenciling, and a linen look. The wide alternating stripes of parsley and light sage green give the room an airy feel. The linen adds texture and dimension to the walls. The stenciled gingko leaves suggest movement, with leaves extending beyond the edges of the stripe. The leaves are designed to be sparse at the top and middle and more concentrated toward the bottom, as if they are falling into a pile below. The technique is shown on a focal-point wall. The other walls are painted in solid parsley green, but they could also be textured with a linen brush.

SKILL LEVEL Intermediate

TOOLS YOU'LL NEED

A

B

C

PARSLEY GREEN SATIN FINISH LATEX PAINT FOR BASE COAT; LIGHT SAGE GREEN SATIN FINISH LATEX PAINT FOR GLAZE COAT

2-INCH LOW-TACK PAINTER'S TAPE

DROP CLOTH

STIR STICKS

PAINT TRAY

STANDARD ROLLER FRAME WITH 9-INCH ROLLER COVER

2-INCH TAPERED TRIM BRUSH

LEVEL WITH PRINTED RULER

WHITE COLORED PENCIL

GLAZE MEDIUM (A)

PLASTIC CONTAINER WITH PRINTED MEASUREMENTS

4-INCH LINEN WEAVER BRUSH (B)

GINGKO LEAF STENCIL, SEE RESOURCES PAGE 191

STENCIL ADHESIVE SPRAY

PAPER PLATE

STENCIL BRUSH (C)

PAPER TOWELS

PARSLEY GREEN AND LIGHT SAGE GREEN LATEX PAINTS

INSTRUCTIONS

Mask ceiling, baseboards, and trim with painter's tape. Paint the entire wall in the parsley green base coat color. Paint two coats if necessary. Leave tape on; let dry overnight.

Measure the width of the wall and divide by the number of stripes desired to determine the width of each stripe. The stripes shown are 24 inches wide. Extend the vertical lines with a white colored pencil and a level. Tape off each stripe with painter's tape.

Mix 4 parts glaze to 1 part light sage green paint in a plastic container. Adjust the ratio if necessary to achieve the desired color for the linen stripe.

1

Roll the glaze mixture onto one stripe. Use a trim brush to cut in where necessary. Working quickly, gently drag the linen paintbrush down vertically from the top of the wall to the baseboard. Repeat the vertical lines until the entire section is done.

2

Starting at the top of the wall and working quickly, drag the linen paintbrush horizontally over the vertical lines. Keep the motions light to avoid completely wiping out the vertical lines. Repeat the horizontal lines until the section is finished. Remove the tape while the paint is still wet; then repeat with the next stripe. Touch up with parsley green paint if bleeding has occurred; let dry.

3

The stencil used for the wall shown is intended as an overall wall stencil, but here it was used to create a random design. Spray the back of the stencil with adhesive and press to the wall. Spoon a small amount of parsley green paint onto a paper plate. Dip the stencil brush into the paint; blot onto a paper towel to prevent bleeding under the stencil. Use a pouncing motion to give the leaves a solid, flat color. Stencil the leaves randomly. The leaves should be sparse at the top of the wall and then pile up at the bottom. Stencil the remaining stripes. Remove tape; let dry.

TIP CRAFTS STORES CARRY SPRAY ADHESIVE MADE ESPECIALLY FOR STENCILS. SPRAY THE ADHESIVE TO THE BACK OF THE STENCIL TO PREVENT THE PAINT FROM BLEEDING AND SMUDGING. ALSO PREVENT SMUDGING BY OCCASIONALLY WIPING PAINT OFF THE STENCIL.

leafstamp

A colorful duvet and pillow shams serve as the inspiration for playfully stamped walls in the girl's room *opposite* and *below*. Leaves are randomly stamped onto a white base color as if they are suddenly falling from a tree. After stamping is complete, a lively lime green glaze is brushed onto the wall, leaving a white outline around each leaf. Minimal furnishings and accessories let the wall design stand out. This design also works well in an upbeat kitchen or bath where bright colors are optional. For a variation, stamp one wall and glaze the other three.

SKILL LEVEL Beginner

TOOLS YOU'LL NEED

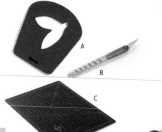

WHITE SATIN FINISH LATEX PAINT FOR BASE COAT; LIME GREEN SATIN FINISH LATEX PAINT FOR GLAZE COAT; DARK PERIWINKLE, DARK PINK, AND MEDIUM PINK ACRYLIC PAINTS FOR STAMPS

2-INCH LOW-TACK PAINTER'S TAPE

DROP CLOTH

STIR STICKS

PAINT TRAY

STANDARD ROLLER FRAME WITH 9-INCH ROLLER COVER

2-INCH TAPERED TRIM BRUSH

STAMP PATTERNS, PAGE 182

FINE-TIP MARKER

SCISSORS

2 COMPUTER MOUSE PADS (A)

CRAFTS KNIFE (B)

SELF-HEALING CUTTING MAT (C)

STENCIL PAINT ROLLER (D)

PAPER PLATE

GLAZE MEDIUM

PLASTIC CONTAINER WITH PRINTED MEASUREMENTS

WHITE AND LIME GREEN LATEX PAINTS; DARK PERIWINKLE, DARK PINK, AND MEDIUM PINK ACRYLIC PAINTS

INSTRUCTIONS

Mask ceiling, baseboards, and trim with painter's tape. Paint the walls with the white base coat color. Paint two coats if necessary. Leave tape on; let dry overnight.

1

The room shown uses two stamps, one 8 inches long and one 6 inches long. Select rubber stamps similar to the ones shown or make your own. To make a stamp, enlarge the pattern on page 182 to the desired size. Cut out with scissors. Use a fine-tip marker and trace around the design onto a mouse pad. Cut the design out using a crafts knife and a self-healing cutting mat.

2

Roll paint onto the stamp with a stencil roller. Apply the stamp to the wall in a random pattern, leaving room for placement of the other stamps. Continue stamping leaf shapes on the wall until the wall is completed.

3

Finish by glazing the walls. Mix 3 parts glaze to 1 part lime green paint in a plastic container. Use a trim brush and brush the glaze onto the walls, leaving white space around each stamp. Work quickly to avoid leaving hard edges that could dry and resemble lines. If you have to stop, feather or brush out the lines where you stop. This softens the glaze edges. When finished, remove tape; let dry.

TIP TOO LITTLE PAINT ON A STAMP WILL PRODUCE A LIGHT IMAGE. TOO MUCH PAINT MAY CAUSE THE STAMP TO SLIDE AND SMEAR.

leafstampvariations

1 The randomly placed leaves in this half bath are double-stamped for a soft, natural look. For this effect, first stamp the leaves in green paint and then stamp directly over them in yellow. If you stamp too many leaves, simply paint over the ones you don't want.

2 A garden of tulips blooms along the baseboard of this wall. Staggering the heights and varying the angles of the tulips creates a natural look. Acrylic paints work well for a project of this size and will cost less than interior paints. After the stamped images dry, add details using artist's brushes.

3 The geometric design in this bathroom is easily created by stamping white paint over a straw-green base coat. The white squares are stamped first, then the remaining green blocks are filled in with white-stamped circles.

1

2 **3**

asianclouds

Express your own creativity by painting a freehand design on the wall. You don't need to be an experienced artist to try this technique. The trick is to first draw the design on the base-coated wall using a colored pencil. When you are satisfied with the results, use a stretchable automotive striping tape to tape along the edge of your lines. Brush an orange-red glaze mixture on the wall using a horizontal dragging motion then remove the tape to reveal the lines, seemingly etched in gold. To increase the richness of the color, apply a dark brown stain to the entire wall. Use this technique to create any linear design or motif that complements your decorating style.

SKILL LEVEL Intermediate

TOOLS YOU'LL NEED

GOLD SATIN FINISH LATEX PAINT FOR BASE COAT; RED SATIN FINISH LATEX PAINT FOR GLAZE COAT

2-INCH LOW-TACK PAINTER'S TAPE

DROP CLOTH

STIR STICKS

PAINT TRAY

STANDARD ROLLER FRAME WITH 9-INCH ROLLER COVER

2-INCH TAPERED TRIM BRUSH

TAN COLORED PENCIL

1/4-INCH PLASTIC AUTOMOTIVE STRIPING TAPE (A)

CRAFTS KNIFE

PLASTIC TROWEL, OPTIONAL

GLAZE MEDIUM (B)

PLASTIC CONTAINER WITH PRINTED MEASUREMENTS

4-INCH CHIP BRUSH (C)

RUBBER GLOVES

AGED OAK GEL STAIN (D)

SMALL PAINT PAN

LINT-FREE COTTON CLOTHS

GOLD AND RED LATEX PAINTS

INSTRUCTIONS

Mask ceiling, baseboards, and trim with painter's tape. Paint the wall in the gold base coat color. Paint two coats if necessary. Leave tape on; let dry overnight.

1

Sketch the design on the wall with a colored pencil. Tape along the edge of the lines with striping tape. Pull gently on the tape to stretch it around the curves, pressing it firmly to the wall as you go. Use a crafts knife to cut the tape to prevent tearing. Burnish the tape with your finger.

2

Mix 1 part red paint to 4 parts glaze medium in a plastic container. Using a 4-inch chip brush, drag the glaze mixture in horizontal strokes across the wall. Work from the top of the wall down. Keep the first coat light.

3

Add paint to the glaze mixture, thickening it to 1 part paint and 1 part glaze. Drag the brush lightly across the surface, varying the amount of glaze and the pressure on the brush to create small patches of heavier color.

4

Remove the tape while the glaze is still wet and repeat Step 3. Let dry.

5

Pour gel stain into a small paint pan. Wearing rubber gloves, apply gel stain to the surface with a clean cotton cloth. Work in small areas, feathering the edges to avoid overlapping lines. Continue until the wall is completed. Remove tape; allow to dry.

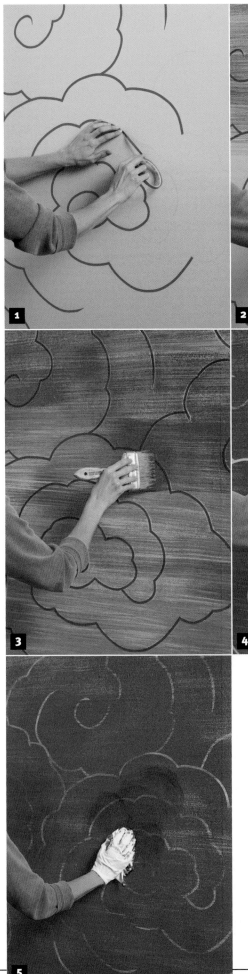

TIPS ALLOW THE BASE COAT TO DRY COMPLETELY BEFORE YOU BEGIN TO TAPE.

TAPER THE ENDS OF THE PLASTIC STRIPING TAPE BY CUTTING THEM AT AN ANGLE. IF THE TAPE STARTS TO PEEL OFF THE WALL, BURNISH IT DOWN WITH YOUR FINGER OR A PLASTIC TROWEL.

LIGHTLY DRAW HORIZONTAL LINES ACROSS THE WALL EVERY 3 FEET OR SO TO HELP YOU KEEP THE INITIAL BRUSH STROKES LEVEL.

free-form vines & linen

The walls of the large sun-filled dining room *opposite* overflow with an elegant hand-painted leaf design. A chair pad serves as the inspiration for the deep red background color above the wainscoting. The wall color and large pattern set off the white wainscoting and trim and dark furnishings. To create this design, draw the vine and leaf pattern onto the wall with chalk. The vines were spaced 15 inches apart to allow for plenty of freedom when drawing the leaves. The leaves were then painted in a golden tan color. To add more depth to the design, use a wallpaper brush to apply dark brown glaze to the wall, giving the pattern a coarse weave similar to a linen look. Use a dramatic design such as this one in a large, airy room that allows the wall pattern to stand out as the focal point.

SKILL LEVEL Intermediate

TOOLS YOU'LL NEED

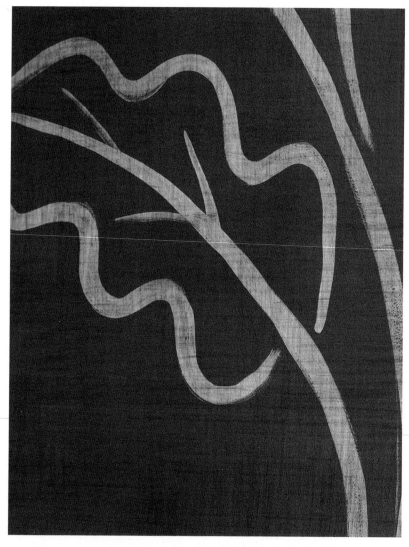

DEEP RED SATIN FINISH LATEX PAINT FOR BASE COAT; GOLDEN TAN SATIN FINISH LATEX PAINT FOR GLAZE COAT

2-INCH LOW-TACK PAINTER'S TAPE

DROP CLOTH

STIR STICKS

PAINT TRAY

STANDARD ROLLER FRAME WITH 9-INCH ROLLER COVER

2-INCH TRIM BRUSH

CHALK

YARDSTICK

LEAF PATTERN, PAGE 183

SCISSORS

LARGE ROUND ARTIST'S BRUSH (A)

LINT-FREE COTTON CLOTHS

GLAZE MEDIUM (B)

RAW UMBER PIGMENT (C)

PLASTIC CONTAINER WITH PRINTED MEASUREMENTS

WALLPAPER PASTE BRUSH (D)

DEEP RED AND GOLDEN TAN LATEX PAINTS

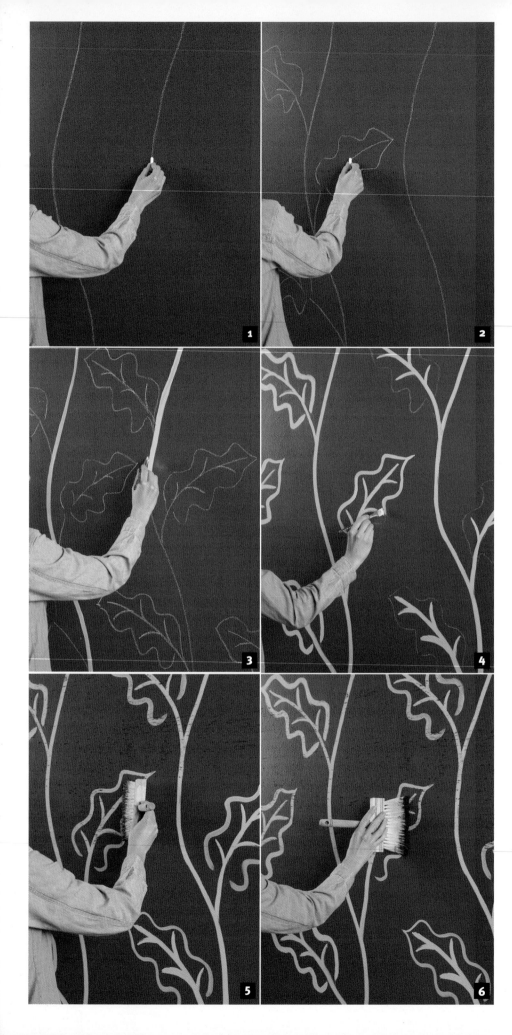

INSTRUCTIONS

Mask ceiling, baseboards, and trim with painter's tape. Paint the entire wall in the deep red base coat color. Paint two coats if necessary. Leave tape on; let dry overnight.

1

Starting in one corner of the room, use chalk to mark points every 15 inches along the ceiling line. Next, mark with the chalk every 15 inches from each ceiling-line mark to the floor. Using these marks as guides, draw a curving line from each ceiling mark to the floor, alternating the curves to the left and right of the points. Try to keep them consistent.

At the second set of points, draw a curved line that is roughly parallel to the first one. Repeat all around the room to create the vines.

2

Use chalk to draw the leaves and stems onto the vines. If desired, enlarge and trace the leaf pattern on page 183 to use as a guide for the leaves. This technique is designed to be hand-drawn, so some inconsistencies are desirable. Start at the top and move down, using the vines as the guideline. Refer to the photograph to assist you with the leaf placement. Adjust the pattern to fit your space as desired.

3

Using a round artist's brush, paint the vines with the golden tan paint following the chalk lines. Work from top to bottom.

4

Paint the leaves and stems in the same manner as the vines. Let the paint dry overnight. Wipe off excess chalk marks with a damp cloth.

Mix 4 parts glaze to 1 part raw umber pigment in a plastic container. Pour a shallow amount of the mixed, tinted glaze into a shallow pan, such as a clean paint tray.

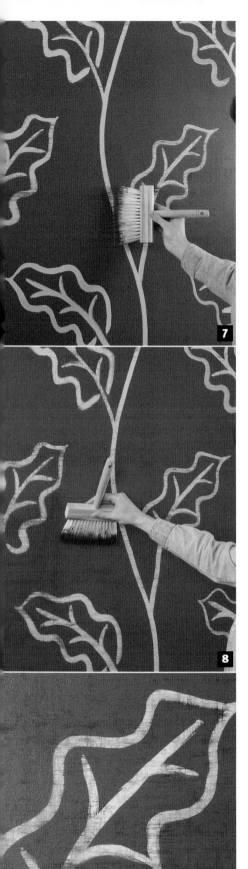

5 6 7

Dip the tips of the wallpaper paste brush into the glaze, picking up a small amount of glaze. Drag the brush horizontally across the wall. Brush back and forth across the same area until an attractive, aged texture is added. The bristles should leave uneven lines that resemble the threads in linen fabric. Reapply the glaze until the wall is covered in horizontal lines. Stagger the starting and ending points of the brushstrokes so no visible pattern takes shape.

Allow to dry.

8

Dip the brush in the glaze mixture and drag it vertically down the wall. Continue until the wall is covered with vertical brushstrokes.

9

Remove tape; allow to dry.

TIP IF NECESSARY, ADJUST THE RATIO OF PIGMENT TO GLAZE TO ACHIEVE THE DESIRED COLOR AND CONTRAST.

decorative motif&recessed panels

Painted decorative panels and motifs like the one *below* became popular all over Europe in the late 1700s. Inspired by motifs found in ancient classical ruins in Rome, the decorations were known as grotesque ornament (from the Italian word *grotteschi* or grottoes). Along with wood graining, marbleizing, and other faux effects, grotesque ornament became a fashionable and popular way of adding color and architectural interest to plain walls. The motifs can do the same for modern rooms, giving ordinary spaces a feeling of formality and sophistication. Although painting the panels and motifs demands patience, do-it-yourselfers can achieve professional results with the patterns found on pages 184–185. Typically the motifs are painted in soft, pale colors, but for a bolder, more dramatic look, you can turn to ancient Roman examples for inspiration. Archaeologists have discovered walls painted in panels of black or red and cream with motifs painted in bright blue, green, and ocher!

SKILL LEVEL Advanced

TOOLS YOU'LL NEED

ANTIQUE-WHITE, GOLD, AND RUST SATIN FINISH LATEX PAINTS FOR BASE AND GLAZES; OFF-WHITE, BROWN, DUSTY BLUE, BRICK, AND SAGE ACRYLIC CRAFTS PAINTS

2-INCH LOW-TACK PAINTER'S TAPE

DROP CLOTH

STIR STICKS

PAINT TRAY

STANDARD ROLLER FRAME WITH 9-INCH ROLLER COVER

2-INCH TAPERED TRIM BRUSH

METAL YARDSTICK

GRAPHITE PENCIL

LINT-FREE COTTON CLOTHS

MINI ROLLER FRAME WITH 4-INCH ROLLER COVER (A)

MOTIF PATTERN, PAGES 184–185

GRAPHITE PAPER

SMALL ARTIST'S BRUSHES (B)

2–3 PLASTIC CONTAINERS WITH PRINTED MEASUREMENTS

GLAZE MEDIUM (C)

ANTIQUE WHITE, GOLD AND RUST LATEX PAINTS, OFF-WHITE, BROWN, DUSTY BLUE, BRICK, AND SAGE ACRYLIC PAINTS

INSTRUCTIONS

Mask the ceiling, baseboards, and trim with painter's tape. Paint the entire wall in the antique-white latex base coat color. Paint two coats if necessary. Leave the tape on; allow to dry overnight.

1

With a yardstick and pencil, lightly mark guidelines for taping off the panels. Our panel is 16 inches wide with a 2-inch frame and 2 inches between the frame and the center panel. The height is determined by the wall height.

2

Use painter's tape to mask off the 2-inch border between the frame and center panel. (For a tip on taping, see "Taping Panels with Success," page 163).

3

Use a plastic container to mix 4 parts glaze to 1 part rust paint. With the trim brush, apply the rust glaze.

4

Use a cotton cloth to blend and soften the glaze, leaving a light wash of color.

5

Use a plastic container to mix 4 parts glaze to 1 part gold paint. Use a mini roller to apply the gold glaze working in one small area at a time.

6

With a cotton cloth, blend and soften the working area. Keep a wet edge so adjacent areas blend together. Let dry; remove tape.

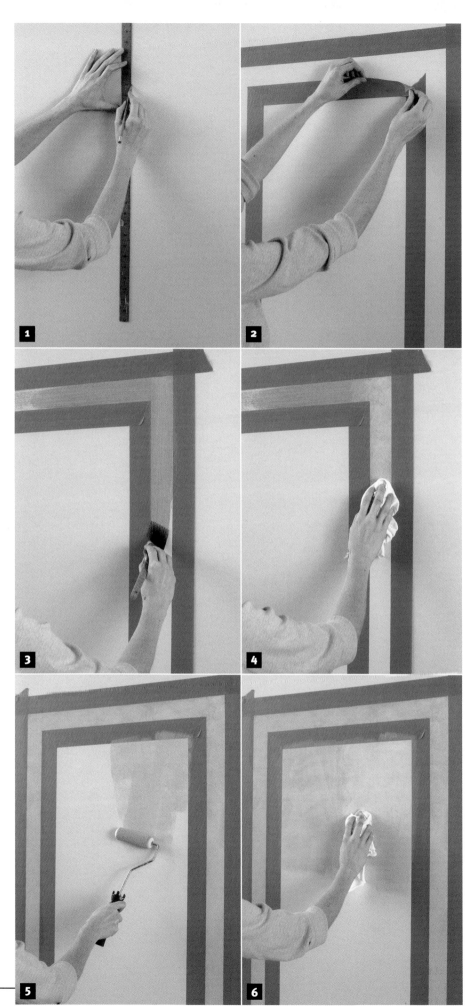

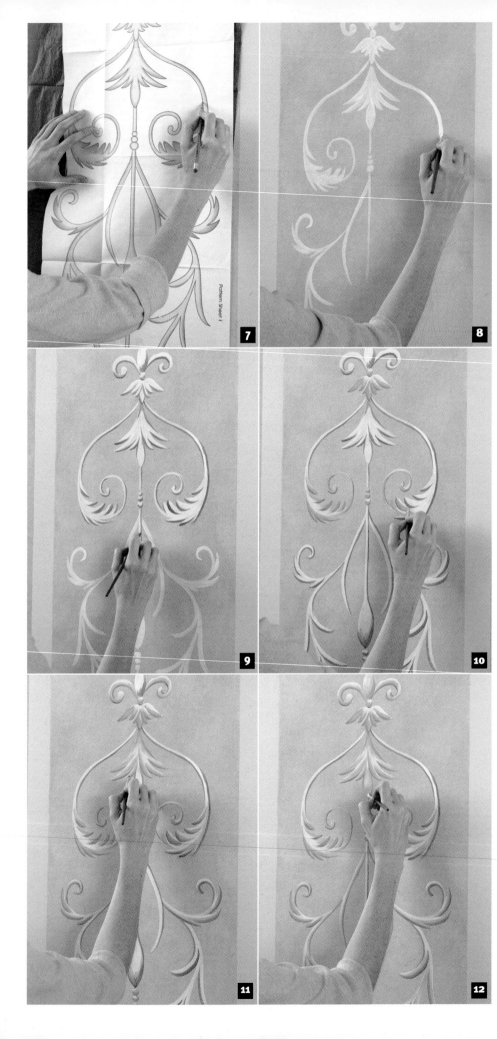

7

Adjust the size of the motif pattern to fit your space. Tape the pattern in place and lightly transfer the design to the desired area using a pencil and graphite paper.

8

Use a small artist's brush to apply off-white acrylic paint to the motif. You may need to add a small amount of water to the paint so it goes on smoothly and lightly.

9

Decide where your light source will be to determine which side of the design you should shade. For shadows and outlines, mix 1 part off-white to 3 parts brown crafts paints. Paint the shadows with a round or flat artist's brush. Use a liner brush for the outlines. Add a little water to the paint if needed so it goes on smoothly.

10

Color-wash selected areas with a mixture of 1 part brick to 1 part off-white crafts paints, using a round or flat artist's brush. When color-washing, go over the shadowed areas lightly to blend colors. Avoid covering areas that should remain as highlights. You also can add highlights with off-white at the end if you desire.

11

Referring to the photo, color-wash selected areas with a mixture of 1 part sage to 1 part off-white crafts paints, adding water as needed.

12

Color-wash selected areas with a mixture of 1 part dusty blue to 1 part off-white acrylic crafts paints, adding water as needed.

13

In a plastic container, thin the gold paint to 1 part paint to 6 parts glaze medium. Lightly glaze

the surface with a cotton cloth to soften and unify the colors. You may stay within the center panel or glaze the entire wall for a soft aged effect.

14
Remove remaining tape; allow to dry.

TAPING PANELS WITH SUCCESS

PAINTING DECORATIVE PANELS INVOLVES A LOT OF TAPING, SO MASTERING THIS TECHNIQUE WILL BE VERY HELPFUL. POSITION THE TAPE ALONG THE EDGE OF THE GUIDELINES AND PLACE THE TIP OF YOUR FINGER WHERE YOU WANT THE TAPE TO TEAR. PRESS DOWN FIRMLY AS YOU PULL THE TAPE BACK, LIFTING UP AT AN ANGLE BEFORE YOU TEAR IT OFF.

fauxpanels

Like the decorative motif on pages 160–163, painted faux panels were popularized by British architects in the 1770s as a means of adding distinction to flat walls. Combining the painted panels with a faux plaster paint finish gives classical grandeur to a room; here the illusion is strengthened by the presence of a real chair rail and molded wainscot. This technique is especially appropriate for public spaces such as dining rooms and formal living rooms. The trick to achieving the effect of three-dimensional molding is to use painter's tape to define a series of slender stripes. These are painted in dark, medium, and light tones to suggest highlights and shadows. Flexible plastic striping tape defines the curved corners inside the faux molding, and patterns allow you to re-create the leaves, medallions, and other ornamental motifs. The old-world texture on the walls between the panels results from applying the paint with a plastic trowel. Faux marble, faux Venetian plaster, or chamois aging techniques would also work well in combination with faux panels.

SKILL LEVEL Advanced

TOOLS YOU'LL NEED

ANTIQUE-WHITE SATIN FINISH LATEX PAINT FOR BASE COAT; RUST, STONE GRAY, BROWN, AND WARM GRAY SATIN FINISH LATEX PAINTS FOR PANELS

2-INCH AND 1-INCH LOW-TACK PAINTER'S TAPE

DROP CLOTH

STIR STICKS

PAINT TRAY

STANDARD ROLLER FRAME WITH 9-INCH ROLLER COVER

2-INCH TAPERED TRIM BRUSH

METAL YARDSTICK

GRAPHITE PENCIL

LEVEL

SMALL PAINT PAN

2-INCH PLASTIC TROWEL

LINT-FREE COTTON CLOTHS

$\frac{1}{4}$-INCH AND $\frac{3}{8}$-INCH PLASTIC AUTOMOTIVE STRIPING TAPE

ARTIST'S BRUSHES

PATTERNS, PAGES 186–187

GRAPHITE PAPER

COMPASS

GLAZE MEDIUM

PLASTIC CONTAINER WITH PRINTED MEASUREMENTS

4-INCH CHIP BRUSH

ANTIQUE-WHITE, RUST, STONE GRAY, BROWN, AND WARM GRAY LATEX PAINTS

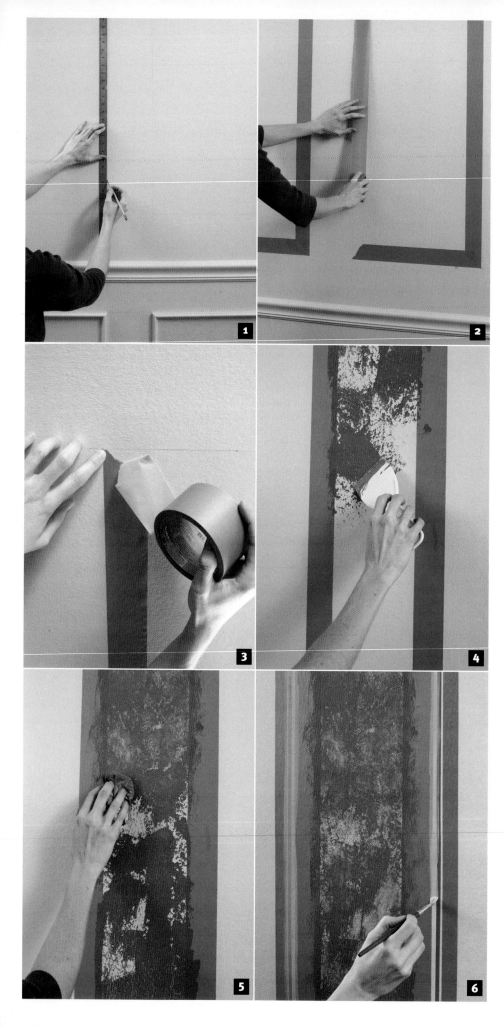

INSTRUCTIONS

Mask ceiling, baseboards, and trim with 2-inch painter's tape. Paint the entire wall in the antique-white base coat color. Paint two coats if necessary. Leave tape on; let dry overnight.

1

With a metal yardstick and pencil, mark the outer edges of the panels. Check your lines with a level. If you are working above wainscoting that has existing panels, use the panels as guides for your layout.

2

Use 2-inch painter's tape to mask off the inner edges of the panels. Burnish both edges of the tape by pressing down firmly with your finger to prevent the paint from bleeding underneath.

3

As you position the tape along the edge of your marked guidelines, place the tip of your finger where you want the tape to tear. Press down firmly as you pull the tape back at an angle before you tear it off. Faux panels require a lot of taping, so mastering this technique will be very helpful.

4

Put a portion of rust paint into a small paint pan. Use a 2-inch plastic trowel to apply rust paint to the wall around the frames. Allow to dry slightly.

5

Rub the surface with a damp cotton cloth to soften and blend the color. Allow to dry completely.

6

Place a strip of 1-inch painter's tape ⅝ inch in from the 2-inch taped edge. Then, within the gap, place ¼-inch plastic tape ⅛ inch from the edge of the 1-inch tape. Burnish the edges of the tape. Brush stone gray paint in the wide gap with a ½-inch flat artist's brush.

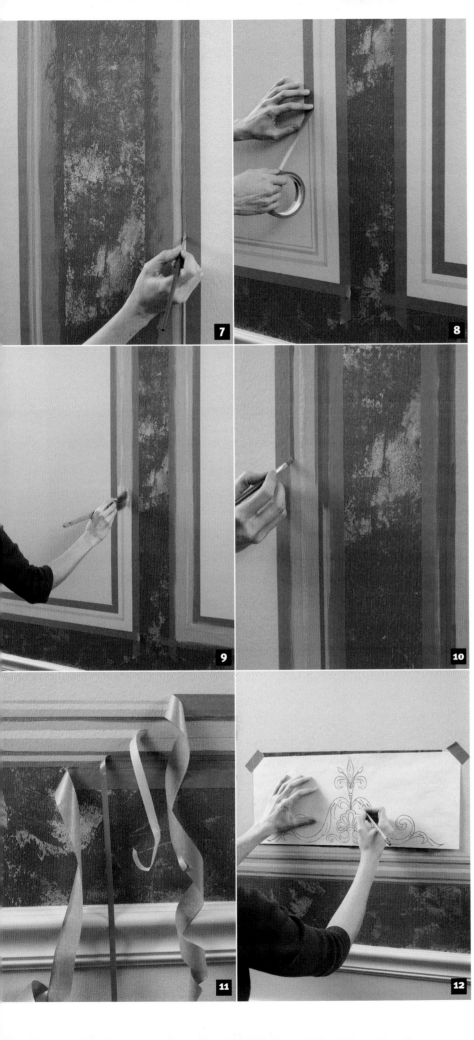

7
Use a ¼-inch flat artist's brush to apply brown paint to the ⅛-inch gap in the tape. Allow paint to dry. Slowly pull off all the tape.

8
Tape off the outer edge of the panels with the 1-inch painter's tape. Place a strip 2 inches in from the outer edge, covering up the rules you've just painted.

Within the 2-inch gap, place a strip of ⅜-inch plastic automotive tape, ½ inch from the edge of the inner 1-inch tape. This tape is shown in light tan.

9
Brush on stone gray paint between the taped edges and painting over the light tan tape with a trim brush. Allow to dry, but do not remove the tape.

10
Place a strip of ¼-inch plastic tape ¼ inch from the outer edge of the panel. With a ¼-inch flat detail brush, apply brown paint within the ¼-inch gap.

Using the taped edges as your guide, brush on a thin strip of brown paint along both sides of the larger gap.

11
Allow to dry. Slowly pull off all the tape.

12
Position and transfer the decorative patterns on pages 186–187 with graphite paper and a pencil. Place the paper between the pattern and the wall with the graphite facing the wall. Avoid pressing too hard with the pencil when tracing. The pattern should be just visible enough to use as a guide.

13
Fill in the design with stone gray paint by using a ¼-inch flat artist's brush. Use a liner brush for the thin lines.

14
Using the ¼-inch flat artist's brush and the liner brush, shadow the designs with brown paint. Add highlights with antique white paint.

Tape off a ⅜-inch-wide rule, 2 inches in from the edge of the frame ending at the designs. Burnish the tape edges with your finger. Use a compass and pencil to create scalloped corners. Brush on brown paint with the ¼-inch flat artist's brush. Allow to dry; remove tape.

15
Mix 1 part warm gray paint with 4 parts glaze medium. Use a 4-inch chip brush to apply glaze to the wainscoting, working in one small area at a time.

16
Rub off and smooth out with a cotton cloth. Keep it somewhat streaky and rough for an old-world effect.

17
Use a 4-inch chip brush to apply glaze over the decorative panels, working in small areas.

18
Rub off and smooth out the glaze with a cotton cloth. Keep it streaky and rough for an old-world effect. Remove remaining tape; let dry.

19
The glaze tones down the contrast between shadows and highlights in the motif.

20 21
Keep the placement of shadows on the motifs consistent for a convincing dimensional effect.

TIPS ALWAYS ALLOW UNDERCOATS TO DRY COMPLETELY BEFORE TAPING.

WHEN ROLLING ON GLAZE, KEEP YOUR AREAS ORGANIC WITH UNEVEN EDGES AND IRREGULAR SHAPES. BLEND WORKING AREAS TOGETHER BY FEATHERING OR FADING THE EDGES. THIS WILL HELP GIVE YOUR FINISH AN OVERALL CONSISTENCY.

USE YOUR FINGER TO BURNISH THE EDGES OF THE TAPE FOR CLEAN LINES. DON'T PUSH TOO HARD, HOWEVER, OR YOU MAY PULL OFF THE UNDERCOAT WHEN YOU REMOVE THE TAPE. TEST AN AREA BEFORE TAPING THE ENTIRE PANEL.

trompe l'oeil

The art of painting walls, floors, or furniture with illusionistic designs is called *trompe l'oeil*, derived from the French term meaning "fool the eye." Trompe l'oeil can be very elaborate, but patterns make the basic design *opposite* and *below* a good introduction to the art. Architectural designs are popular themes for this type of hand-painted artwork, and embellishing a plain, arched doorway with a painted molding and keystone adds instant character. The secret to effective trompe l'oeil architecture is using light, medium, and dark tones for the shadows and applying them in a sequence that mimics true cast shadows. (The instructions that follow indicate which tone to apply and where to apply it to create the darkest shadows, medium shadows, or highlights.) Start with the keystone at the center to ensure that the molding around the arch and down the sides will be evenly balanced.

SKILL LEVEL Advanced

TOOLS YOU'LL NEED

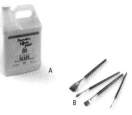

WHITE SATIN FINISH LATEX PAINT FOR BASE COAT; PALE GOLD SATIN FINISH LATEX PAINT FOR GLAZE COAT; LIGHT TAN, MEDIUM TAN, AND DARK TAN ACRYLIC CRAFT PAINTS

1-INCH AND 2-INCH LOW-TACK PAINTER'S TAPE

DROP CLOTH

STIR STICK

PAINT TRAYS

STANDARD ROLLER FRAME WITH 9-INCH ROLLER COVER

2-INCH TAPERED TRIM BRUSH

PATTERNS, PAGES 188–189

GRAPHITE PAPER

GRAPHITE PENCIL AND COMPASS

METAL YARDSTICK

GLAZE MEDIUM (A)

2-3 PLASTIC CONTAINERS WITH PRINTED MEASUREMENTS

SMALL PAINT PAN

MINI ROLLER FRAME WITH 4-INCH ROLLER COVER

LINT-FREE COTTON CLOTHS

ARTIST'S BRUSHES (B)

¼-INCH PLASTIC STRIPING TAPE

WHITE AND PALE GOLD LATEX PAINTS; LIGHT TAN, MEDIUM TAN, AND DARK TAN ACRYLIC PAINTS

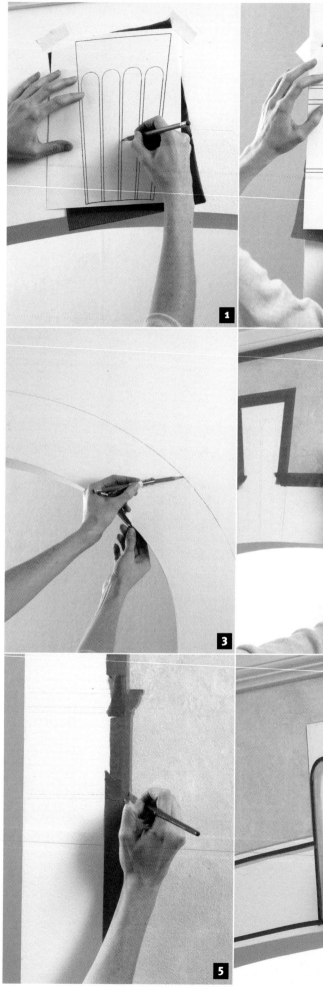

INSTRUCTIONS

Mask ceiling, baseboards, and trim with 2-inch painter's tape. Paint the entire wall in the white base coat color. Paint two coats if necessary. Leave tape on; let dry overnight.

1
Use a yardstick to find the center of the arch and lightly trace the keystone pattern with the graphite side of the paper facing the wall.

2
Position the side pattern with the top approximately 5 feet above the floor. Transfer the pattern to the wall using the same process as for the keystone pattern.

3
Hold the metal edge of the compass on the inside of the arch and use a pencil to mark a 5-inch-wide guideline connecting the side and keystone patterns. Use a metal yardstick to draw the sides.

4
Apply 1-inch painter's tape along the inside of the lines. Burnish the edges of the tape by pressing down firmly with your finger to ensure a sharp, clean line. Mix 1 part pale gold to 4 parts glaze medium in a plastic container. Use a 4-inch paint roller and small paint pan to apply the glaze on small sections. Lightly rub off and soften the glaze with a cotton cloth. Let dry.

5
With a ¼-inch flat artist's brush, apply a line of dark tan along the right edge of the arch and side. Apply medium tan along the top of the arch and left side for the outer shadows. If the light source comes from the right, reverse the colors. Let dry; remove tape.

6
Place a strip of ¼-inch plastic tape approximately ⅜ inch from the outer edge of the arch and along the outer edges of the small flutes

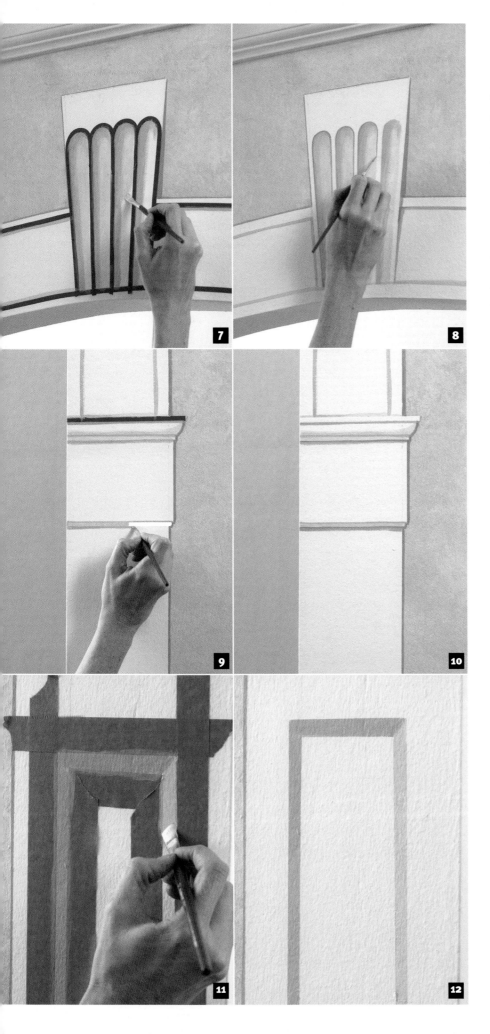

in the keystone. Burnish with your finger to ensure clean edges. Use a ¼-inch flat artist's brush to apply a slightly watered down mixture of dark tan along the top and left sides of the flutes.

7
Using a ¼-inch artist's brush, apply a slightly watered down mixture of medium tan in the center of the flutes. Brush on a mixture of 1 part light tan to 1 part medium tan to the inside right edges of the flutes. With the same brush, apply medium tan along the inside edges of the tape on the arch. Allow to dry; remove tape.

8
Enhance the shadows with undiluted dark tan paint applied with a liner brush.

9
Apply tape for clean edges. Use medium tan mixed with light tan for the lightest shadows, medium tan for the medium shadows, and dark tan for the darkest shadows. Enhance the shadowing on the side motifs, using a liner brush.

10
The completed side motif should have the appearance of sunlit shadows.

11
Create the inset panels on the inside of the arch by taping off a ⅜-inch-wide frame with 1-inch painter's tape. Burnish the inside edges with your finger. Brush dark tan on the top and left side of the frame and a mixture of 1 part medium tan to 1 part light tan to the bottom and right side of the frame. If your light source is coming from the left, reverse the left- and right-side colors, leaving the top and bottom colors the same. Allow to dry; remove tape.

12
The final inset panel should appear recessed.

wallgraphics

Give your walls a fun, contemporary facelift in less than one hour by using wall graphics. These oversize geometric designs are self-adhesive and easily ahere to painted walls and ceilings. Before you begin, plan your design on paper or tape the shapes to the wall. When you're ready for a new look, simply peel them off. Wall graphics are available in various shapes and sizes (see Resources page 191). They are perfect for bedrooms, baths, and teen retreats.

SKILL LEVEL Beginner

TOOLS YOU'LL NEED

LIGHT BLUE FLAT FINISH
LATEX PAINT FOR BASE COAT

2-INCH LOW-TACK PAINTER'S TAPE

DROP CLOTH

STIR STICK

PAINT TRAY

STANDARD ROLLER FRAME WITH
9-INCH ROLLER COVER (A)

2-INCH TAPERED TRIM BRUSH (B)

GRAPH PAPER

GRAPHITE PENCIL

WALL GRAPHICS, SEE RESOURCES
PAGE 191 (C)

HARD RUBBER SQUEEGEE (D)

ADHESIVE TAPE

LIGHT BLUE LATEX PAINT

INSTRUCTIONS

Mask ceiling, baseboards, and trim with painter's tape. Paint the walls in the light blue base coat color. Paint two coats if necessary. Remove tape and let dry overnight.

1

Decide on the proper placement of the wall graphics. Sketch out a design using graph paper to help you visualize the scale and placement of the pattern. Use adhesive tape to test the design by temporarily taping the graphics into position on the wall.

2

The graphic is sandwiched between a clear transfer sheet and a white backing. Lay the graphic down on a hard flat surface with the white backing side face up. Firmly rub the squeegee over the entire surface. This secures the graphic to the clear transfer sheet.

3

Peel the white backing off and place the graphic on the wall in position with the transfer sheet face out. Use the rubber squeegee to burnish the graphic to the wall surface.

4

Gently and slowly peel the clear transfer sheet off by pulling at a 45-degree angle. If the graphic starts to lift off the wall with the transfer sheet, re-burnish the graphic and continue to peel.

5

Continue this process until your design is complete.

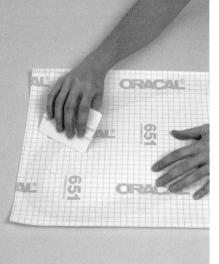

TIPS ONCE THE BACKING HAS BEEN REMOVED, DO NOT ALLOW THE ADHESIVE SIDE OF THE GRAPHIC TO FOLD BACK ONTO ITSELF.

MAKE SURE YOUR WALL IS SMOOTH, DRY, AND DIRT-FREE BEFORE APPLYING THE DECALS.

ornamentalappliqué

Easy-to-apply wood appliqués allow you to transform plain windows and walls with the look of elegant 18th-century carved trim. Painting the trim to match the walls emphasizes the textural effect—and creates a subtle elegance. There are two ways to adhere the decorative corner pieces. A handheld steamer activates the glue in each piece, or you can use good-quality wood or construction glue to secure them. Lay the design out on graph paper before you begin. Since the design is subtle, you can use larger decorative pieces.

SKILL LEVEL Advanced

TOOLS YOU'LL NEED

CREAM SATIN FINISH LATEX PAINT FOR BASE COAT

2-INCH AND 1-INCH LOW-TACK PAINTER'S TAPE

DROP CLOTH

PAINT TRAY

STIR STICK

STANDARD ROLLER FRAME WITH 9-INCH ROLLER COVER

2-INCH TAPERED TRIM BRUSH

GRAPHITE PENCIL

METAL YARDSTICK AND LEVEL

BRISTOL BOARD OR HEAVY PAPER

SCISSORS

MITER SAW

TRIM MOLDING AND APPLIQUÉS, SEE RESOURCES PAGE 191

WOOD GLUE

HAMMER, SMALL TRIM NAILS, AND A NAIL SET

SPACKLE

SANDPAPER

LINT-FREE COTTON CLOTH

ELECTRIC STEAMER (OPTIONAL)

PRIMER

CREAM LATEX PAINT

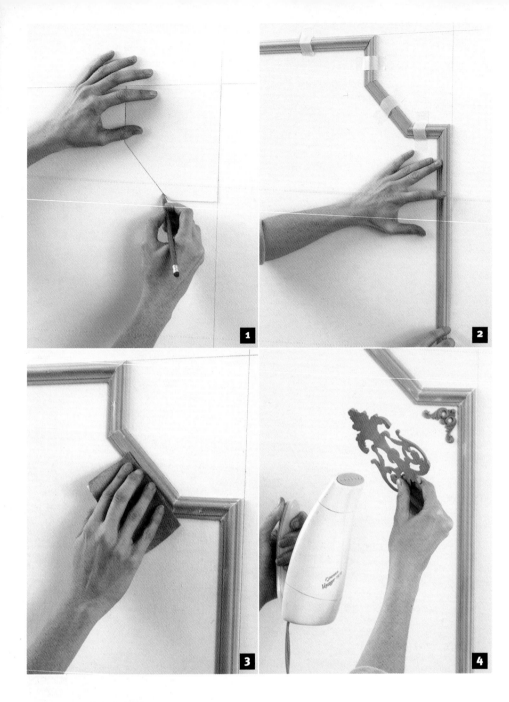

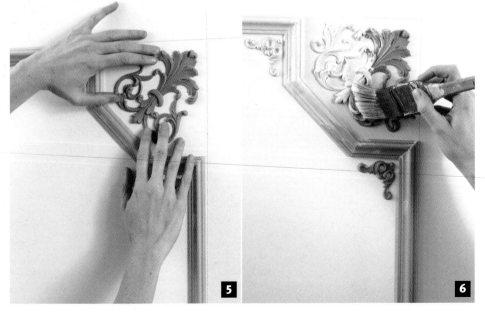

INSTRUCTIONS

Mask ceiling, baseboards, and trim with 2-inch painter's tape.

If your walls are not already a light, neutral color, paint the entire wall with the cream base coat color. Paint two coats if necessary. Remove tape; let dry overnight.

1

Determine the layout of the decorative appliqué pieces and the placement of the trim molding. Use a pencil and yardstick to mark off the outer edges and corners where the trim molding will be. Check the lines with a level. Use scissors to cut a piece of heavy paper or Bristol board according to the diagram *opposite bottom*. Place the board in each corner you've marked off and trace the angled edges to use as guidelines.

2

Cut the trim molding to size. It's a good idea to cut a test corner first to ensure the angles will meet correctly. (See tips for cutting the trim molding provided in the diagram *opposite bottom*.) Glue the trim molding to the wall, lining it up with the inside edge of your guidelines. Use 1-inch painter's tape to hold the trim in place until it dries.

3

Nail the trim securely and set the nails using a nail set. Spackle the corner joints and holes; let dry. Sand lightly and wipe clean with a dry cloth.

4

Apply the emblem pieces using one of two methods. Use a handheld steamer to activate the glue in each piece before placing it into position, or use any quality wood or construction glue to adhere the pieces to the wall. Use painter's tape to hold the pieces in position until the glue has set.

7

5

Use the outer corner of your guidelines to position the large appliqué at a 45-degree angle then apply the smaller side pieces. Remove tape; let dry.

6

Prime the molding and decorative pieces using a 2-inch trim brush. You may need to lightly sand the wood trim molding after it has dried to ensure a smooth surface before painting the base coat color.

7

Apply the cream base coat color to the entire surface.

8

Allow to dry.

TIP IF YOU USE A GRAPHITE PENCIL TO MARK THE POSITIONS FOR THE MOLDING, KEEP THE LINES LIGHT SO THEY WON'T SHOW THROUGH THE PAINT.

8

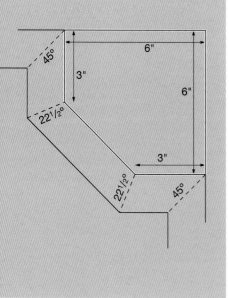

antique embossed walls

Create the look of antique wainscoting on your walls. Start by applying embossed wallpaper in any pattern. Wipe a mixture of paint and glaze over the wallpaper and into the crevices with a cloth. Then wipe off some of the paint using a handmade squeegee. Add a row of ceramic-tile trim to complete the antique look. Select your paint carefully: Latex paint mixed with glaze will clean up more easily, but oil-base paint with glaze provides a longer and more flexible working time—and a more washable surface after the paint dries.

SKILL LEVEL Beginner

TOOLS YOU'LL NEED

A

B

C

D

E

BLUE-GREEN SATIN FINISH LATEX PAINT

2-INCH LOW-TACK PAINTER'S TAPE

DROP CLOTH

STIR STICK

PAINT TRAY

STANDARD ROLLER FRAME WITH 9-INCH ROLLER COVER

2-INCH TAPERED TRIM BRUSH

LEVEL WITH PRINTED RULER

BLUE COLORED PENCIL

EMBOSSED WALLPAPER (A)

GLAZE MEDIUM (B)

PLASTIC CONTAINER WITH PRINTED MEASUREMENTS

LINT-FREE COTTON CLOTHS (C)

CERAMIC-TILE TRIM (D)

HOT-GLUE GUN AND STICKS (E)

BLUE-GREEN LATEX PAINT

INSTRUCTIONS

Mask baseboard and trim with painter's tape. Paint the top half of the wall above the chair rail in the blue base coat color. Paint two coats if necessary. Leave tape on; let dry overnight.

Mark a level line 30–34 inches from the floor. If your wallpaper has a specific pattern, such as the grid shown, adjust this line to fit the wallpaper pattern.

1

Hang the wallpaper from the line down according to the manufacturer's directions. Mix 2 parts paint to 1 part glaze in a plastic container. Apply the mixture to the wallpaper by using a damp cloth, rubbing the mixture into the crevices.

2

While the paint is wet, wrap another clean, damp cloth around a paint stir stick to create a squeegee.

3

Run the stir stick over the surface, removing the paint from the raised areas but leaving it in the crevices. Change or rinse the cloth when it becomes saturated.

After the wall is completed, remove tape and allow to dry.

Apply a narrow row of ceramic-tile trim along the upper line with a hot-glue gun.

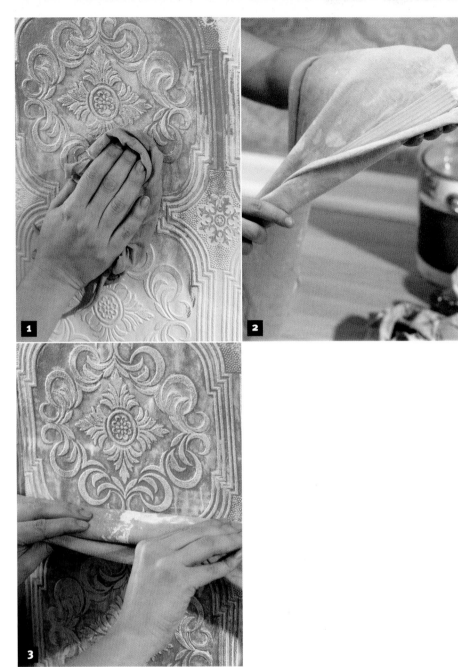

TECHNIQUE 38
simple curved stencil
Page 138
Shown at 85%
Size to fit your space

TECHNIQUE 42
leaf stamp
Page 150
Shown at 65%
Size to fit your space

TECHNIQUE 37
flower & vine stencil
Page 136
Shown at 70%
Size to fit your space

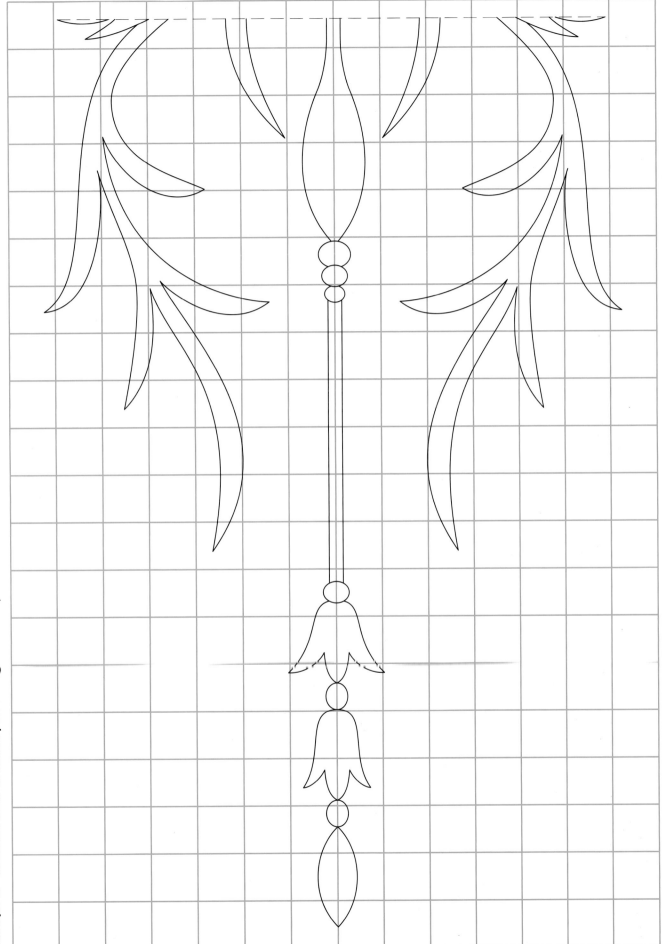

TECHNIQUE 46 faux panels Page 164 1 Square=1 Inch

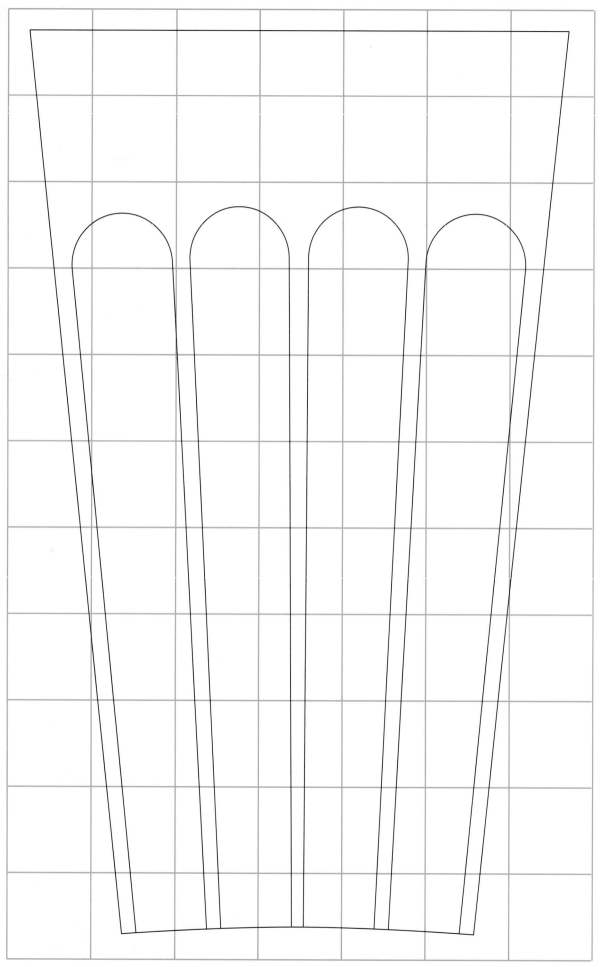

TECHNIQUE 47 **trompe l'oeil** Page 170 1 Square=1 Inch

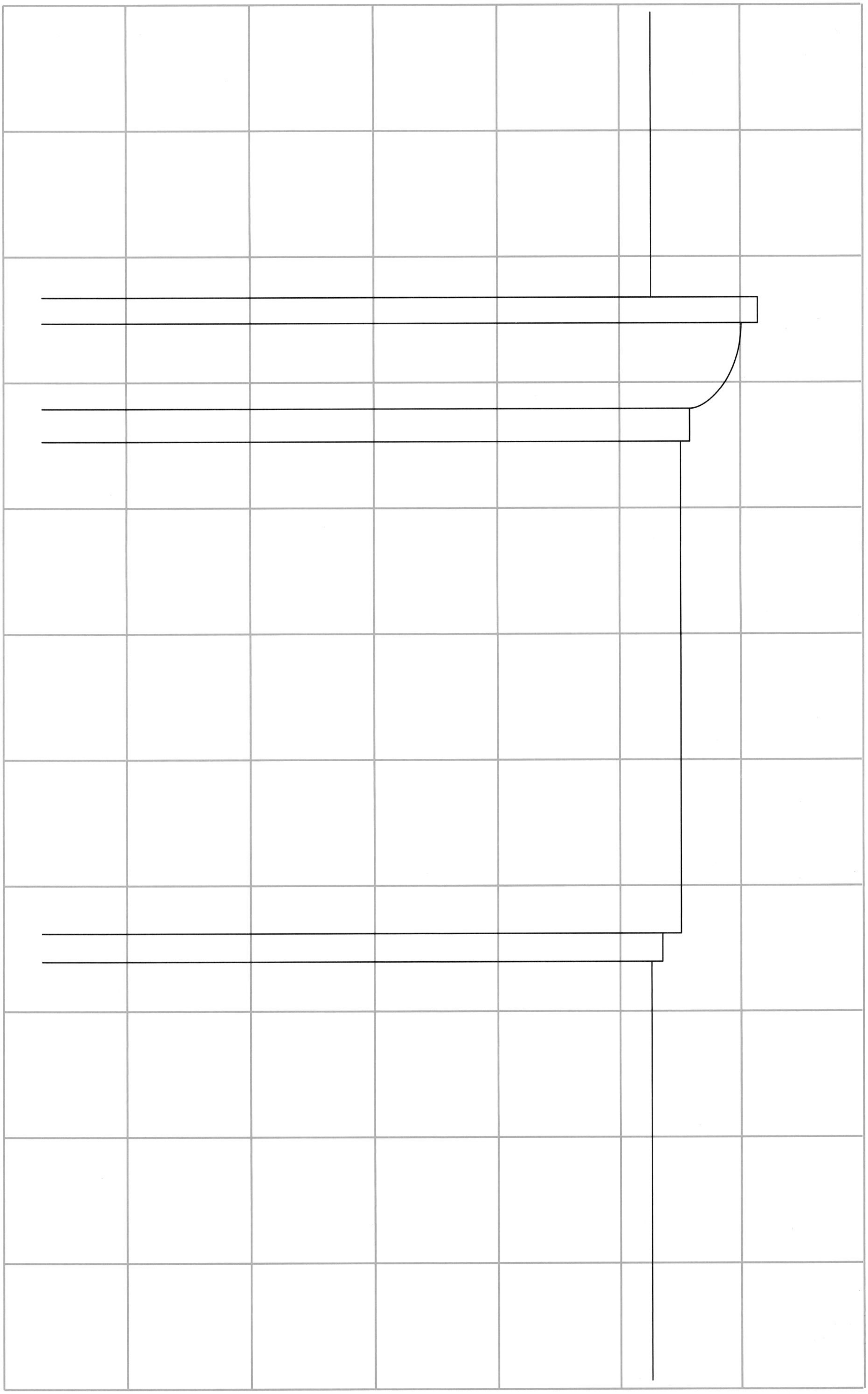

Find Your Style

Better Homes and Gardens
Decorative Painting
STEP-BY-STEP

Better Homes and Gardens.
decorative PAINTING MA EAS
BONUS SECTION
ACTUAL-SIZE
TECHNIQUE
SAMPLE

- **More than 25 faux finishes and paint techniques**
- **Step-by-step instructions**
- **Ideas for every room**

Better Homes and Gardens.
decorating ideas under $50
quick updates
to what you
already own

Better Homes and Gardens
color schemes made e

Better Homes and Gardens.
COLOR WITH CONFIDENCE
YOUR ROOMS, YOUR WAY

Better Homes and Gardens®

The elements of your style...
can be found in great decorating books from
Better Homes and Gardens®—wherever books are sold.